# Christians Helping Christians

# Christians Helping Christians
*Chistian Coaching In A Secular World*

By
William Perry, Th.D., Ph.D.

Endorsement:


Bill,

This is beautifully done. Well organized. You provide a lot of good insight and practical thought for the Christian Life Coach.

Lots of good material about physical care, good eating practices.

Solid instruction at the beginning as you define and explain the role of the Christian Life Coach.

Useful material for those struggling with death and grief.

Useful material for all who might pursue Christian Life Coaching.

Dr. Glenn Mollette,
*President of Newburgh Theological Seminary and College of the Bible.*

# Table of Contents

# ACKNOWLEDGEMENTS

The writing of this book was made possible with the help and support of Dr. Glenn Mollette. I also want to give thanks to my Sons, Jim and Eric, as well as my daughter Jennifer, who have been a great encouragement to me in this pursuit. I want to thank Pastor John Duchardt for whetting my appetite for the Word of God, many years ago. To both Jack Wyrtzen of "Word of Life" ministry, and Jerry Farwell of Liberty University, for their encouragement in my walk of Christian Service. All three have now been promoted to Glory, and are home with their Lord. I also want to thank my wonderful wife, Kathy, for her continued encouragement, guidance, patience, suggestions, and continual assistance and support. Without her this endeavor would not have been possible. Most of all I want to thank my Lord Jesus Christ for calling me into this work.

# CHRISTIAN LIFE COACHING
# IN A SECULAR WORLD

## Introduction

"When you start out on the journey you think it is all about taking in experiences to fulfill yourself. But it's not. The greatest experience is changing someone else's experience of life, and once you come to that realization, it becomes your foundation, the ace in your pocket, who you are… When you see the world through the lens of others, that's when you find yourself." (Andre Agassi) [i]

In the Holy Bible, Peter's writings provide a clear picture of our role as believers in Christ. In the Holy Bible, 1 Peter 2:9, Peter writes, "But you are a chosen people, a royal priesthood, a Holy Nation, God's special possession, that you may declare the praises of Him who called you out of darkness into his wonderful light."[ii]

Yes, we as Christians are a royal priesthood, given the privileges and obligations of carrying out the ministry of Jesus Christ. Although, unlike what we know of the Old Testament-era priests, we do not wear elaborate robes and hats, nor do we sacrifice animals to God on an altar. Today we do not serve in the temple. Instead, today, we are called on to communicate the message of Jesus Christ, that He is the one who became the supreme sacrifice for us (Hebrews 9:27-28).[iii] We serve as a living sacrifice, in our bodies of flesh and blood – not buildings of brick and mortar. As a believer in, and a follower of Jesus Christ, our body is the temple of the Holy Spirit (1 Corinthians 3:16-17).[iv] Today, we offer a new kind of sacrifice; we offer our very lives in service to Christ (Romans 12:1-2).[v] Today, we have now, been entrusted with ministerial responsibility of building up the body of Christ (Ephesians 4:16).[vi]

It is for us to be encouraged, as we affirm, and are affirmed that it is God Himself who is seeking us to participate in this grand adventure of serving Him, by; celebrating, supporting, and developing other leaders for the Christian community. As we consider our calling, we must be aware that ministry is not something we hold on to like an old pair of riding boots that is useful only to one person. But ministry is meant to be shared with others, so that the effects and impact can be multiplied, many times over. The joy of ministering to others is what truly makes the ministry of coaching so rewarding. As a coach one may well be in a position to influence others, who, in turn will be able to affect the lives of many; family, friends, and others. As you become involved as a Life Coach, your potential impact on others is limitless, as the Lord sees fit to multiply the effect of your ministry, as you serve Him as a Christian Life Coach, injecting hope and truth into the hearts and lives of many.

God has uniquely created and designed every individual, as ones created in His image, to display facets of His character in their being, and to enact His love through their activities. He has gifted each of us with unique passions, reflecting more than enough to motivate us in His service. Through our many experiences throughout our life, He has provided various means of preparation in His calling us to a life mission that provides real joy, as a by-product of giving our lives to His larger purposes.

Each of us has been designed for a purpose; God has a great purpose for each of us who are called by His Name. As a Christian Life Coach, we are called to help discover His path for ourselves, and encourage others to seek, and live out their unique destinies, so, they can better serve the Kingdom and love the King in the process. As we consider the many needs of today; never before has there been a greater need, for life coaching, and even more so, in Christian life coaching.

## The Lord's Call:

In the Lord's service, be it the Pastorate, the Foreign Mission Field, Coaching, or Sunday School Teaching, the Lord doesn't usually call anyone to easy jobs. Just look around, try finding someone who ever felt competent for the demanding service God has called him or her to. Being called into the Lord's service is a mighty call, and not to be taken lightly. Show me a person who feels fully competent on his/her own strength, and I will show you a person who might be advised to question his/her call a bit farther. We must consider Moses, and remember that he trembled as he was called. Mary was troubled, as she considered her family, her betroved (Joseph), she was troubled; not understanding what was ahead for her. Paul was more than just a little troubled, Paul was terrified! As he lay flat on his back before the Lord Jesus, after being thrown off his horse while on his way to Damascus, he was terrified. We can see from Moses, Mary, and Paul, and there are many other examples, as we look through the Scriptures that the Lord's call is demanding. "Callings" rattle cages and rock boats. Callings shatter illusions of complacency, and erase the thought of easy life and comfort. Callings often shake the status quo to its very foundation. Callings startle, confuse, provoke, and prod to the very depth of the soul. At times, those who are called are overwhelmed, reluctant, and mystified, holding on for dear life, saying, "No, not me! You must have someone else in mind, someone who can speak better, someone who is more connected, who is smarter, faster, and more spiritual." A call into the Lord's Service may be, and often is, costly to the one who is called. Call it fear, wisdom or reluctance to the call of the Lord, it may be, humanly speaking, truly understandable, but, to be sure, prayer, trust and acceptance is far better.

Now, if your call into the Lord's service moves you just a bit to the right or left, outside of your comfort zone, welcome to the fellowship of the amazed and reluctant, and the humble. You can be sure that you have just had your name placed alongside of many others of the reluctant, the amazed, the humble, who answered the call with a YES; Abraham, Moses, Ester, Paul, John Wesley, Peter Cartwright, Moody, and many others, myself included with the ones who never felt up to the task. You have been invited to join the club. (1 Cor. 9:16; 2 Cor. 3:4-6; 2 Cor. 4:7-12; 2 Cor. 12:7-10.)[vii]

As we humble ourselves, as we heed to His calling, we are reminded, that it is the Lord who is doing the calling, and as the one who calls, as we respond to His call, He is also the one whom we can and must depend on to equip us, in order that we might fulfill His call. We are to take confidence, therefore, that, as He has been Faithful in the past, so He is "Now", and on into the "Future", He will continue to be Faithful. The Lord Jesus Christ will work in us to finish the task He has started.

**PRAYER:** Perhaps, before you continue, it is the time to take "Time out" with the Lord, for Prayer; for strength, for direction and encouragement, as you continue, as you follow Him into the unknown. Knowing that when you get there, He will be waiting for you; trust Him with your every step, with your very life- Amen'.

# WHAT IS A LIFE COACH?

In the words of teacher, counselor, and bestselling author, Gary Collins, Ph.D., "A Life Coach is in many ways, very similar to the consulting that has become popular in business and some church circles in recent years. Usually consultants are paid to analyze a situation and give expert guidance and advice. We once attended a church that had grown beyond its capacity but had no place to expand. A paid consultant was hired to analyze our situation give suggestions about what we should do. He talked to church leaders, gave a detailed questionnaire to the congregation, looked carefully at the community, and then gave his analysis and recommendations in return for his consulting fee. Often we need experts like this. If you are sick, you go to a doctor for a consultation about your physical condition and its treatment. In business, a consultant might analyze existing problems and practices, suggest better marketing and business strategies, and help companies improve performance and develop future plans. The consultant is an expert who analyzes and makes recommendations."[viii]

As we ask the question, "What is a Life Coach?" We get the following words from Ralph Waldo Emerson, "Our chief want is someone who will inspire us to be what we know we could be."

As we attempt to clarify what life coaching is, it is important that we define what the art of general coaching is. In our search, we find the art of coaching, for the most part, can be defined as; helping people grow in their abilities, without telling them what to do. To be even more precise, a coach is a change expert, one who will help others take the responsibility for their own desires and acts, and help them maximize their potential.

We do need to understand from the start, that coaches are not to tell and direct, but instead, the coach is to use his or her understanding, training, and genius, to envision and communicate, to believe in people, and bring a perception of need together with desire, to mix this all together with the dynamics of human potential, thus, bringing this together in unity, pointing out options and opportunities.

# WHAT IS THE IMPACT OF LIFE COACHING?

As we examine the impact of Life Coaching, we find a number of differences, ways, and practical benefits life coaching can make in a life.

1) To help us understand a life purpose. This understanding produces a sense of meaning and significance, provides a foundation for making great decisions, and offers direction for how to live a purposeful life.

2) Helps us to align our lives with core values. This tends to increase life satisfaction, reduces stress and frustration as we do what's important instead of what's expected or what life thrusts upon us.

3) Eliminates tolerations. This frees the energy needed to pursue important goals in life, while increasing our joy on the journey.

4) Allows us to identify and overcome internal obstacles. Helps us get unstuck and allows us to move forward, and provides the freedom we've always wanted from nagging fears and self-doubt.

5) With this freedom, we can create a life purpose action plan. It creates real movements toward our life purpose, with the sense that our life is truly going somewhere.

6) We become open to the clarity of hearing God's call. We obtain greater obedience to our Lord, intimacy in our relationship with Him, with greater impact for the Kingdom of God.

7) God's guiding hand in your life is revealed. It produces wonder, peace, love and worship for your Creator.ix

A good description of a Coach may be defined as being an expert at helping others shine in their quest. Who do you think is the better boxer, the fighter or the trainer? Who do you think is the better truck driver, the cross country driver with his years of experience or the teacher? Who is the better rider, the jockey or the riding coach? So, who would be the better CEO, the personal life coach or the person actually leading IBM, or Ford Motor Company, Intel, or Microsoft? I believe, you see where I'm going with this. Coaches are not necessarily the world's best leaders, or managers, but to be sure, they may well be in a position to help the best, become even better. And for the life coach, personal success may truly be found in releasing others to succeed.

### Asking Questions:

A personal life coach should seek to take seriously the art of becoming a master in the art of asking questions. It is suggested that you schedule yourself into a 10 to 12 week exercise program, to tone up any flabby asking muscles you may have. It's your program, but a suggestion may be, a self-study work-out, or, perhaps, a session with a peer coach, who will help to increase your proficiency in asking coaching questions. Also, you may want to practice, using a phone, each week, for around 60-75 minutes, or, until you are able to ask probing questions, engaging others in life decision answers. You may also want to work out in a peer session where you practice on each other, along with one exercise to try out on your own during the week with a friend, family member or client.

Questions have power, and can change lives. In using the right questions, you are likely to be able to jump-start creativity, change a perception, empower people into believing in themselves, push someone to think things through, or, call them to action.

As a life coach, in order to engage the situation and learn ways that may better able you to meet the needs of the client, you are encouraged to seek to improve your store-house of asking tools in ways that will strengthen your ability to meet each moment in your coaching conversation, with powerful, incisive questions.[x]

A good coach will be a person who will help a client find their untapped potential within. That may mean getting through the day productively, or, it may be preparing for, and setting up a new, or, redirected, course for your life, that will make a difference; coaching in the direction of fulfilling God's plan and purpose for life.

# WHAT IS A CHRISTIAN LIFE COACH?

The definition of Christian Coaching can be expressed by this simple equation of Christ's Vision and Mission, which is:

> Scriptural Principles
> + Christ's Presence
> + High Standard of Excellence as a Trained Coach
> = CHRISTIAN COACHING

Christ Centered Coaching is coaching that is focused on promoting Biblical Christian discovery. Christ-Centered coaching additionally utilizes the power of the Holy Spirit in focusing on that discovery process. The design is in helping the client focus on their untapped potential within themselves. A coach should guide the client to discover that potential, and what needs to be done; allowing the client to use his/her wants, desires and experiences to come into play. The coach does not provide the answer, make the decisions for the client, nor tell them what to do. A coach will help the client find answers, rather than provide answers. Unlike Job's friends (Job 11: 1-5)[xi] who had all the answers, a coach will listen and ask questions in order to help guide the client in finding the right answer for him or her to consider. Have you ever attempted to talk with a friend about a situation you may have concerns about, but you find that even though your friend may be well intentioned, like so many, what he wanted to do was "fix it". His suggestions were to immediately find a solution to the problem so it would just go away. And as you thanked your friend, you no doubt left, after your conversation, rubbing your chin, being even more frustrated and misunderstood than ever. Your friend may have had the best of intentions, but, I must clue you here, that is NOT the way a good coach works. A coach must be someone who truly listens with intentions of hearing, trying to understand the client's needs. And now, in the process of listening, you are able to begin to evaluate answers that are developing in your head that you convey for your client to consider. And in doing so, you are assisting him/her in coming closer to meeting their goal.

It is safe to say, just as some who are involved in counseling, or as consultants are Christian- yet others are not. It is also safe to say, that some professional coaches are Christian, and some are not. Sad to say, some Christian counselors, consultants, as well as coaches do not choose to work from a Christian worldview perspective.

I would state at this point, that my worldview is Christian, and all that I am, and what I do, including coaching, is Christian. My coaching is centered in the Holy Bible, and on the personhood and precepts of Christ.

The Bible lets us know in Psalm 139:14-16, "I will praise You, for I am fearfully and wonderfully made; marvelous are Your works, and that my soul knows very well. My frame was not hidden from You, when I was made in secret, and skillfully wrought in the lowest parts of the earth. Your eyes saw my substance, being yet unformed. And in Your Book they all were written, the days fashioned for me, when as yet there were none of them."[xii]

## The Work of a Christ-centered Coach:

I would like for you to consider the times when you were encouraged to do a little research of your own, to discover an answer you were searching for, rather than being given the answer you may have had a bit of difficulty finding. I would like for you to think about how that experience helped you as you headed down that path, continuing on toward your life goals. At this point, you might want to set aside a little time, and ask a discovery question of someone you know (a question they will have to search for, to research), be it a child, a friend, or a ministry colleague. Now, take notice how they respond to the question, and to their finding. Were they frustrated in not receiving an answer from you, or, were they inspired by the answers they received through their own effort? Now, use this experience to consider how your response to a question might be similar or different? Next, consider how you might use this experience/insight to make coaching even a better experience as you assist your clients?

*Song of Solomon 2:14*
"... *Let me see your face, let me hear your voice...*"[xiii]

Jesus the Christ Himself is truly the Master Coach; we would do well, first of all, to understand that Jesus was one whose very life changed history, and it was not only because He was the Son of God, and to be sure He was and is the Son of God. It was also, because as He spoke, His voice was a unique voice, not just an echo of others. He did not just perpetuate the way things had been done, but He let us know that we were to "Do it differently." He did not intend to remind others what had been said in the past, He spoke out with words, such as, "Behold, I show you a new way of doing things... things that have never been done before."

Today, as never before in the history of the world, many in our contemporary world have lost their voices, and have been duped into surrendering themselves to television, radio, the Internet and the endless array of talking heads on the boxed-in portions of TV screens that are telling us what we should be doing, thinking, or acting. And today, we are even invited to view the continuous bits of "news" as the little craw strips perpetually stream across the bottom of our media screens. Their purpose, of course, is to provide us with information about the perceived state of the world around us. And It goes on and on, seemingly, endless amounts of information, alerting us to our world's problems. It seems to me that for every one person who is talking, there are others shoving microphones in the face of the one talking, asking, "Can you tell us something we don't already know?"

As we watch the world around us, we may ring our hands over the mass amounts of information, depicting the moral decay of our society, through hours upon hours of this media onslaught, at times we neglect to realize, that, we, must also be fed from the Word of God, and now, as we study the Bible, allow ourselves to be transformed from the ways of the "world", the ways of God (Romans 12:1-2).[xiv]

As we look into the Bible we can find the answers. We must slow down, turn off the many collective electronic media systems, open the Bible and take the time to read. The words found In Romans, Chapter 12:1-2 are, "I beseech you therefore, brethren, by the mercies of God, that you present your bodies a living sacrifice, holy, acceptable to God, which is your reasonable service. And do not be conformed to this world, but be transformed by the renewing of your mind that you may prove what is that good and acceptable and perfect will of God."[xv]

It is now, we are to investigate ways of measuring success in God's economy. We also, should become aware of what God's economy is not. Success in God's economy IS NOT, falling in step, or falling in line with the world of new information technology, that is changing on a daily basis. Yet, unknowingly, many today define success in these very counterproductive, and, or, unbiblical ways.

One common trap we submit ourselves to, is, by measuring ourselves against others.  When we try to measure ourselves against others, it is now that success becomes relative, as such; success now becomes an elusive moving target, instead of something that may be attainable to each of us.  In considering success in this way, some may expect to feel certain feelings as they observe the outward signs perceived to spring from success.  Depending on their perception of success, they may feel all problems in life should magically disappear, if they are really faithful Christians.  And still others may measure success in terms of outward religious behavior instead of the heart, i.e.: "I know that I am a success if I do everything right, or pray enough, or practice the right disciplines."  To be sure, an unbiblical picture of success can cause one a lot of heartache.  This, by the way, is a very good reason to have a good understanding of the Bible.  It is very useful, as a coach, to have a solid grasp of Scripture, and be aware of how success is defined by God's perspective.

**Stewardship:**

In God's perspective, success has a simple standard, and this standard fits very well into the coaching methodology of today.  In the Kingdom of God, success is all about stewardship; about making the most of what you have been given.  The parable of the talents,[xvi] for instance (Mt. 25:14-30), teaches us that we are all stewards of our own lives.  We are responsible for taking good care of God's gifts.  This means taking some risks, and stretching ourselves, to use our abilities, rather than letting them lie dormant.  The "Master" rewarded the servants who fully used whatever they had been given, and criticized the one who wasted opportunities.  The "Master" never compared the servants with each other; instead, comparing their results to the resources they'd been given.  (This also provides a real imperative for their life purpose discovery; how can you effectively steward what you've been given when you don't even know what you've been given?) Have you ever taken the time for an inventory of God's gifts?

To God, success has to do with who you are. To God, success is more about becoming the right kind of person than doing all the right things. Success to God is fulfilling our inward potential as someone created in the image and likeness of God, this is what enables us to do what we were created to do. We should remember that "Doing flows out of being", James 2:17, "Thus also faith by itself, if it does not have works, is dead."[xvii] Real success is about who we are.[xviii]

# BECOMING A CHRISTIAN LIFE COACH

It is not uncommon to find that for many of the ones who are considering becoming a life coach, in some way, are in search of significance, meaning, they are looking for a sense of their life being more worthwhile, working toward doing something meaningful with their life.  At this point, it is important to understand how this search for significance fits very snuggly and nicely into a biblical worldview.  As we continue to view the teachings of Jesus, we easily see that He had a keen insight into what is truly significant in life. His idea of the meaning of life is so profound it can be expressed in a single word: Agape!  The center of His teaching regarding life, was, and is, to love God with all your heart, soul, mind and strength, and to love your neighbor as yourself (Luke 10:27).[xix]  It is well at this point, to keep in mind the various reasons for wanting to be involved in Life Coaching.  It is because Life Coaching is what makes life work.  The most significant life possible, for anyone, is a life of freedom and power to offer another the gifts of love, justice, compassion, service, peace, and kindness to everyone you meet, without the need to get something back.  That is Agape love, a Godly love.  Imagine, if you will, having the freedom of living out that kind of overflow of God's love, into a full life of helping others. Helping others obtain a life free from any hang-ups of craving for security, significance, or acceptance, un-entangled by anger and inner wrestling's, with the pouring out of internal resources in ways that would always be available to those around you.  Now, you have to agree, that would be a great life to live.

### Who are my Heroes?
One of the best ways to explore life's significance is to ask; who

are my heroes? What do I find about them that made their life significant? Also, while you are looking, look at characters of the Bible, at times, this will draw people to want to learn more about their lives, in detail.

It was our Lord Jesus who showed us that aligning our life with loving, giving and serving is truly the path of significance. Since the desire for significance is a major factor in driving people to seek a coach, it may be well to begin a preparation to think in terms of an opportunity, and, to grapple with the possibility of a life created around love, instead of one around recognition, accomplishment, or personal fulfillment. It really is better to give than to receive.

*"Vision leads the leader. It paints the target.*
*It sparks and fuels the fire within. Show me a leader without vision,*
*and I'll show you someone who isn't going anywhere".*
*(John C. Maxwell)*

**Leading With Vision:**
To become a good leader, vision is the important difference, and today, as never before, visionary leaders are in very short supply. The church hungers for leaders with vision, as does the corporate world, as well as the government of our country. If you are gifted in your ability to help people through the course of life, to find a clear vision and a way to help them move in the direction of their perceived goals, then you are well ahead of the pack in your quest of becoming a life coach. If you are willing to take it upon yourself to apply a few of the vision-finding principles to yourself, you can benefit greatly, in having a much greater understanding of what your clients are seeking to accomplish.

On that long ago, and, fateful day, when Moses fled Egypt for parts unknown (at the time), fearful of his life, with his tail between his legs; at the time, he thought any purpose for his life was now past. You remember, it was after identifying with the Hebrew people, and their plight, Moses, almost, at once, attempted to use his Egyptian royal power and position to seek for their welfare. After all, he was of the Pharaoh's royal household. He was well trained in the ways of Egyptian leadership, with standing in the Egyptian court, he was a man completely prepared to intercede on their behalf. Of all the known Hebrews of his day, he was the only one who had been born and raised to rule. All the others had been born into slavery. It was Moses who knew the Egyptian society inside out. Of the Hebrews, who else was better qualified to lead? He was strong, tall, educated, with a large supply of confidence in himself. But, Moses was missing one very important element to be successful in his task, what he needed was; not more confidence in himself, he had too much of that already, what he needed was confidence in God. For the next 40 years, God would see that a radical change would be in store for Moses, as he would learn through humility, hard work and responsibility to transfer his trust, from self-confidence to God-confidence.

As stated by Jack Welch, while he was chairman and CEO of General Electric, "Confidence gives you courage and extends your reach, it lets you take greater risks and achieve far more than you ever thought possible."

## Confidence:

Looking into the requirements of a life coach, we can understand that confidence in God is very important, as is the quality of being a person of character. Confidence is one of the attributes that gives us the needed inner self-assurance we will need to properly interact with others. It helps to equip us with the deep belief that we can

live out our perceived life purpose. Without this confidence, we will
have a tendency to pull back and hide. Without this confidence,
our tendency may be to give up on ourselves, or, in God's power to
work through us. Over the past number of years, we may have come
across certain self-help gurus who have suggested that confidence is
built upon certain little tricks, such as posture, dressing for success,
the right tie, a strong handshake, powerful cologne or deodorant,
or having an image consultant. They want us to believe that
confidence is a matter of looking right and acting in a way that will
give the impression that you know what you are doing. But, with
this understanding of what confidence is, we have a big problem, and
the problem we have is; with all this "Acting as if"; what happens on
your "bad hair day?" what happens when you don't think you look
right? What happens when you forget to see yourself as confident?

No, the answer is not make believe, nor is it play acting, true
confidence does not come from believing in yourself, but from
putting your faith in The Lord Jesus Christ, and believing in Him,
placing your complete faith in Him. As we look at confidence even
deeper, we will see that in the true sense, pervasive self-confidence is
not at all self-confidence, but God-confidence. This is another one
of those Spiritual paradoxes, like losing your life is finding it, or the
last shall be first. You see, real confidence is only as good as the one
in whom this confidence is placed. You get involved in trying really
hard to work up your confidence by going to your barber, getting a
shave or a haircut, changing your hair style at the beauty shop, or a
new suit of clothes, or perhaps, putting on a dazzling smile. You can
be assured that your confidence may well be short lived, and only
last as long as you can maintain that smile, or your new suit stays
shinny clean. This effort could all be destroyed by a rainy day or bad
breath.

It is evident that if real confidence is what you're looking for, it will be very important for you to place your hope and trust in God Himself. This radical shift is necessary, from self-confidence to God-confidence, and one that will make all the difference. Sociologists are quick to let us know their perception of what is called self-esteem. They tell us, it is all based on who we believe to be the most important person(s) in our life, and what that person(s) thinks about us. If that were to be a fact, and you've learned to pick up your self-esteem cues from someone other than God; a parent, a best friend, a mate, or maybe even the books you choose, or your self-talk, your confidence will suffer each time you get a negative message from any of these. You should be looking to God for your self-esteem cues. As you do, how much more will you be able to see how solid and unshakeable your confidence becomes? As you trust the Lord, you will become more and more aware of who you are in Him, despite what anyone might say- and despite what you might tell yourself. You discover that you are worthwhile; you are lovable; you are acceptable; you are desirable; you are forgivable.

## Life Experience:

In our varied experiences in life, often, God trains us through these experiences in the very skills and character of the destiny He has prepared for our life and what that requires. This may take place in ways and locations that may seem totally disconnected from what we might even imagine the Lord has been training us to become. We remember how Moses' struggle was very much intensified, as God began to put the finishing touches in his preparation for what lay ahead. First of all, God had to remove him from his comfort zone in Egypt, and move him into a position and at a location very much like his ultimate role would be. Moses had to be demoted into a much smaller area of influence before God would bring him into an even greater influence of being the leader of the Hebrew people.

Because Moses did not really recognize or understand what his ultimate destiny would require of him, in the way God was preparing him for leadership and character, in a way that would be required of God in his preparation for leadership.

Just consider, if you will, for a moment, regarding a few of the many things Moses learned during his years of living in tents, living in the dry arid land, herding Jethro's sheep, protecting the flock, and learning, learning and learning some more. Because he was destined to lead a group of slaves who'd lived along the Nile for 400 years, it was now, after the many years of training, that Moses was the only one of the Hebrews who knew:

1. How to survive in the desert.
2. Where the roads were and how to navigate through the trackless wastes.
3. Where the springs and the oases were.
4. Where the best grazing for cattle was at different times of the year.
5. What desert plants could be eaten by people, and animals.
6. The wild animals found in the desert, and how to handle them.
7. What the local customs were.
8. Where the forts and guarded places were.[xx]

One of God's requirements was, somebody who had a well-rounded education in desert survival skills. That is, if all of those slaves were going to have a chance at survival in that very unfamiliar environment; God had chosen Moses to be that someone to perform that task. Maybe Moses turned out to be a slow learner, but I don't believe so, there was much to learn. It took him a full forty years of training to learn the many basic skills of desert leadership and to use the practical desert skills that would be needed. During this time in his life, Moses was involved in this unique form of training, in character training, as well as lessons in humility and utter dependence on God. In fact, everything in Moses' life, from the circumstances of his birth to his upbringing, to his years tending sheep, fed into his calling. Moses' whole life was spent preparing him for what he was born to do; lead the Hebrews into the Promised Land.

# JUST WHO IS A LIFE COACH?

From the lips of Olympian, Jesse Owens, "We all have dreams. But in order to make dreams into reality, it takes an awful lot of determination, dedication, self-discipline, and effort." What has God been preparing you for?

**Making Ready to Serve:**
As we take an in-depth look at God's preparation, and how valuable it is for anyone whose preparation is in the process of taking place outside of their area of call, it is now, through life's experiences, or other means of preparation that the Lord leads us in, and eventually, through our training process, in preparation for His call on our life. When a CEO, of a major company is called to start a branch in a small 3rd world country, or, when a Pastor of a mega church is called to plant a church in a small, rural farming community, when a farmer who has never worked any other place other than the farm he was raised on, is sent to the mission field, each one may struggle to feel adequate, in doing what their hearts are calling them to do.

The story from the Bible, of Joseph, is a good example; this is a classic example of outside preparation. After being dropped into a pit, betrayed by ones he trusted and forced into slavery in a foreign land, spending time in a dungeon prison, he is now, after taking, no doubt, a cold, shower, cleaning himself up with a quick shave, he was snatched out of that dungeon, and called to stand face to face, before the most powerful man in all the earth, at the time—The mighty Pharaoh. Now, I want you to consider here, how you would have perceived this young man, should you have had been the one to look at his resume', along with his past working experience, up to this time in his life. I'm pretty sure you would have considered him to have limited possibilities. Having available, only what you could determine from the information at hand at the time. I'm afraid you would have no choice but to agree that this young man was totally unprepared for the task that was just ahead of him. But, if you could have had the ability to look deeper into his character and integrity, and if you were able to see Joseph from God's perspective, you would see that he had been trained well, and he had learned well also. As we know, his character and wisdom were made evident to the mighty Pharaoh, by the much mightier God, so that, Pharaoh, instantly trusted him and gave him the full reins of the entire Egyptian economy.

We must consider that it was God that was the true confidence and security for Joseph, confidence and security that obviously were so desperately needed for the great responsibility of God's call on his life that lay ahead, and now, moved him directly from a dim, dark, dungeon society, directly into his call as a national leader. "God does not call the trained, but trains the called"- Author unknown

We have learned of other well-known leaders, of whom God placed large callings on their lives, how they have been required to go through some major moving and shaking, as well as going through some unusual experiences early in life. Even to the point of experiencing, what may seem to them, earth shattering, at the time; life changing catastrophic illness, being falsely accused, living in or working under abusive conditions, or suddenly finding themself leading an organization that is on the verge of falling apart. This may well indicate that it is a time to "Trust in the Lord with all your heart, and lean not on your own understanding." (Proverbs 3:5)[xxi] Because, in reality, the Lord may be preparing you to be fit for the great task He has prepared just for you.

A calling is about serving Christ for the good of others. Preparation to serve others is not just a function of skills; you also have to become the kind of person that people in the area of influence will look to. You can have all the right answers and the best educational credentials, but if no one is listening, you won't have any influence.

Another way of putting this truth, is, that skills channel character. The eternal content of what people receive when you serve them in the Christ that is in you—the act of service is just the channel for it. The true power of service is not that you fixed my roof when I was in the hospital. It's that someone actually cared enough about me to love me in a practical way. And so I receive the heart of Christ through the service.

The better your outward skills, the more people are impacted by the heart of Christ behind them. Ministry takes the Christ incarnate in you and channels that embodiment through your skills, strengths and abilities to others. Ministry is something you are, something that comes out through what you do. Because the heart is such an important part of presenting Christ to the world, much of a leader's preparation involves embodying Him in character qualities like, dependence, trust, humility, love, and grace. But since most people think of preparation almost exclusively in terms of skills, credentials and work experience, reframing life experience around character preparation can lead to huge breakthroughs.

In his book, <u>Christian Life Coaching</u>, Tony Stoltzfus gives us a list of "Preparation Principles" in helping us to understand the varied ways God uses to develop leaders. Below are some guidelines we may want to use, as some of the best perspective questions for understanding the principles of how God develops leaders. These are varied examples of preparation principles that often occur in the lives of developing leaders:

1.  God will take you through experiences that help you identify those you are called to serve. For instance, if you are called to minister to the grieving, your own grief will prepare you for that task.

2.  Many of your experiences build the faith and fortitude muscles you'll need to succeed in your calling. Dealing with the annoying people in your office builds the skills and character to deal with human needs on a larger scale.

3.  Failure is as good a preparation as success. If your calling involves revitalization of dying organizations, what better preparation than to be a part of an organization that dies— or better yet, to lead one?

4.  Often God has to exercise a lesser love in your life to make room for you to embrace His greater purpose. Having your company go belly up is an excellent way to become detached from pursuing material things.

5.  When God deals with a leader, everyone who serves under that person also gets dealt with. The adversity may be primarily about someone else's preparation. Are you willing to pay a price for their destiny?

6.  Your place of power in ministry is where God has most deeply dealt you your character—because that's where Christ is most fully incarnate in you. For instance, if you are called to teach leadership skills, expect God to put your own leadership under a microscope and hold you to an unfairly high standard compared to others.

7.  God often gives leaders a glimpse of their call early in life, but then there is a long season of inward preparation in relative obscurity before they emerge into the call. For a thirty something client who feels stuck in that middle

season, it always helps to look at the times of Abraham, David, Joseph, Paul, or even Jesus.

8.  God will not allow you to go to your call from a place of security, where all your needs are met. Your destiny will require faith for God's provision,

9.  Big leadership challenges early in life can be an indicator of a large sphere calling.

10. Graduating successfully from a certain stage of your preparation is usually marked by removal from that sphere or facing a larger challenge. Endings don't mean you've failed. God wouldn't give it to you if He didn't think you were ready for it.

11. A wilderness season is a mark of special affection from God. He leads us into the desert to draw us into deeper intimacy with Him. (Hos. 2:14-16)[xxii]

## A Destiny Event:

When you have a sense of knowing something about your life purpose, you are better able to connect your preparation experiences together with your destiny. This helps, in many ways, as you work with people, you are likely to become somewhat more aware of their purpose, and how the Lord may be involved in that purpose. As we become more aware of this, we can see that a destiny event may well be a brief experience where we sense we are doing the kind of thing we were born to do. We may hear this described as a time when they were "doing something that brought out my best." These experiences are generally associated with:

1.  A sense of fulfillment, significance and a deep satisfaction.

2.  Heightened effectiveness or exceptional impact.

3.  Strong affirmation from others that this is you.

**Overcomer:**

I hope you are aware that as a Christian, you are an overcomer. Do you not know that? I do hope you believe that. Do you not know that everything you need to be victorious is available to you? As one who is indwelt by God the Holy Spirit, you are a winner. Some of you may see this statement, and say to yourselves, "At this time in my life, I sure don't feel much like an overcomer". Or maybe a few of you thought that you actually do NOT have what you need to be victorious. Others have come to a conclusion, that if the battle has already been won, why am I not seeing it? Allow me to convince you, by sharing a bit from the life of just one of my many Bible heroes, Gideon. His story is found in Judges 6-8. Reading though Judges 6 (specifically, I direct your attention to verses 11, 15, 27, and 36-39).[xxiii] I encourage you to open your Bible, and read this portion, and as you read, you will get a snapshot of Gideon's personality. Here The Bible lets us know that, "Gideon was beating out wheat in the winepress to hide it from the Midianites." He says, "My clan is the weakest in Manasseh, and I am the least in my father's house." But because he was too afraid of his family and the men of the town to do it by day, he did it by night. As we Read through Judges 6, it is easy to conclude that Gideon was a man full of fear, insecurity and doubt. Yet when an angel of the Lord appeared to Him in Judges 6:12, this angel did not address Gideon as "Scaredy Cat", "Weakling" or "Loser". He said, "The Lord is with you, O mighty man of valor." But it's just like Gideon to pay no attention to the fact that a heavenly being is right in front of him calling him a "mighty man of valor!" It seems that he immediately disputed the angel's statement by listing all of the reasons why that could not possibly be true: "And Gideon said to him, 'Please, sir, if the Lord is with us, why then has all this happened to us? And where are all His wonderful deeds that our fathers recounted to us…

But now the Lord has forsaken us and given us into the hand of Midian.'" (Judges 6:13).

Because Gideon didn't see it, he could not believe it. The Gideon we find here in the first half of his story is one man, and to be sure, we now find a changed man, a very different man than the Gideon we see in the second half. "And Gideon returned to the camp of Israel and said, 'Arise, for the Lord has given the host of Midian into your hand.'"[xxiv] (Judges 7:15) "'Well then, when the Lord has given Zebah and Zalmunna into my hand, I will flail your flesh...'"[xxv] (Judges 8:7) "...and he pursued them and captured the two kings of Midian, Zebah and Zalmunna, and he threw all the army into a panic." [xxvi] (Judges 8:12) Whoa! Where did this bold, faith-filled, strong man of God come from? What happened in between Judges 6 and Judges 7:15 to bring about such a dramatic shift? One minute he is quivering in fear, the next he is touting about how he will destroy any who come against him? Did he lose his mind? Did he get a lobotomy? Nope, neither, the only thing that changed was that Gideon started to get a glimpse of who God actually is, and to believe what God said about him. You see, one step of faith led to another, and before we know it, Gideon was walking in the authority the Lord had proclaimed on him back in Judges 6. God saw Gideon as a "mighty man of valor" well before Gideon had seen it himself. Once he started to believe it, it was now, he began to see it.

In the same way, if you believe that Jesus is the Son of God, and have placed your life in His hands, God calls you an overcomer! "For everyone who has been born of God overcomes the world. And this is the victory that has overcome the world—our faith. Who is it that overcomes the world except the one who believes that Jesus is the Son of God?" [xxvii] (1 John 5:4-5)

**Walk in Faith:**

We are to walk by faith, and not by sight, and as we begin that walk by faith (and not by sight), we become overcomers. As we start to believe what our Heavenly Father says about us, what Jesus says we can do, and what the Holy Spirit Himself testifies He will do through us, we become overcomers. As God said to Gideon, "Do you understand that I am the One sending you?" [xxviii] (Judges 6:14) As we hear the Voice of God, we no longer have to rely on our strength alone. Our mighty Deliverer is with us to fight our battles. Our job is to stay the course, to stay close to Him and let Him do what only He can do. It's at this point I encourage you to read through Judges 6-8 today, or as soon as is reasonable for you to do so. Learn from Gideon. Walk by faith, not by sight, trust in what God says, and let your Father fight your battles!

John says in 1 John 4:4, "Little children, you are from God and have overcome them for He who is in you is greater than he who is in the world." [xxix]

As a well-known bestselling Christian leadership author says, "Leaders must be close enough to relate to others, but far enough ahead to motivate them."xxx  John C. Maxwell

If you were to be able to get close enough to God, to climb up on his lap, and tell Him all the things that are running through your mind, right now, what would that list look like? Now, as you're sitting there (on God's lap), take all the time you need, make that list, and don't be shy, but let go, be exhaustive. After all, remember, God already knows the desires of your heart. Hold on, don't neglect to include anything physical you even want, and don't neglect anything. Remember to list that new power tool, how about an in-ground swimming pool, or that new 4x4 pick-up truck you've been looking at. How about a handy man to keep the yard up, to trim your hedges? Just write this all down, just do it! Now, take some time to review your list and place an "N" next to items that seem to represent genuine needs, and a "W" next to items that are, truly just wants. What do you observe about your list when you identify your needs and your wants? And now, circle the items that seem to be causing you anxiety, conflict, or envy. If you are sacrificing peace of mind, forfeiting relationships, forgoing giving to others, or focusing your thoughts and energy on those things, then they could be enslaving you.

Have you ever noticed how attractive an activity looks, that is, until you actually have to do it day after day? No matter whether the activities of your day energize you or irritate you, fascinate you or frustrate you, you can be content in what you do by changing why you do them, and for whom you do them. "Whatever you do, work at it with all your heart, as though you were working for the Lord and not for people."[xxxi] Colossians 3:23

Ask yourself, "What is preventing me from my life goals?" And without further adieu or delay, start moving forward, devoting the needed effort to that end, improving your resolve to reach out, trusting the Lord for your needed resources!

# WHAT A LIFE COACH IS NOT

For one thing, Life Coaching is not for those who need therapy to overcome disruptive painful influences from the past; it is for relatively well-adjusted people to build vision, and move forward, toward the future.  Coaching is not reactive looking back; it is proactive looking ahead.  It is not about healing; it's about growing.  It focuses less on overcoming weakness and more on building skills and strengths.  Usually coaching is less formal than the therapist-patient relationship, and more of a partnership between two equals, one of whom has skills, experiences, or perspectives that can be useful to the other.

Former Chairman and CEO of General Electric said, *"In the future, people who are not coaches will not be promoted."*[xxxii]  *-Jack Welch*

Dr. Gary Collins, in his book, Christian Coaching, writes, that, one day he received an e-mail suggesting that "the term coaching is the going word for the personal mentoring movement" and that "one-on-one discipleship is not far apart from Christian coaching, except perhaps the terminology."  The writer suggested that we drop the word coaching, and use the word discipleship instead.  Others have suggested that coaching is a new word for counseling and that any of these words might be replaced with such terms as modeling, spiritual guidance, and soul care, or brief-strategic therapy.[xxxiii]

As a group of church leaders had gathered for the purpose of discussing a name, or a term that would describe this "new" direction that had come forth to help people see the life ahead that the Lord has laid out for them, many suggestions had come about.  About this time, it seems that a young pastor, during a breakfast meeting, suggested still another term. He said, "I don't need a father, I have a good dad, I don't need a counselor, but if I wanted one I would know where to turn. More than anything else, I need somebody to journey with, somebody who has walked the road of life a little longer than I have. I want someone to come alongside me for an hour or so every week, to talk about life, I want to learn from your experiences, and have you help me avoid some of the potholes on the road." From that, the breakfast meeting was changed, and was called "our journeying time together".[xxxiv] What we need is someone to walk with us as we make this journey through life. As a Life Coach, we may be in a position to assist in that life journey.

## A Rose Is A Rose:

But really, does it truly matter what name we use for our activity? I for one believe that it does. Coaching most certainly overlaps other activities such as; counseling, mentoring, and discipleship. All of these activities involve relationships in which at least one person is further along in the journey of life and is willing to guide others, often as a trusted role model. All of these terms involve accountability, encouragement, and a commitment to growth. Despite the overlap, however, we can assume that coaching is a unique process involving skills and assumptions that differ from the other specialties.

"For surely I know the plans I have for you, says the LORD, plans for your welfare and not for harm, to give you a future with hope. Then when you call upon me and come and pray to me, I will hear you. When you search for me you will find me; if you seek me with all your heart, I will let you find me." [xxxv] – Jeremiah 29:11-14a

Dr. Gary Collins, in his book, Christian Coaching, lets us know that Christian coaching is not a replay of high school football!

Even the term Christ-Centered coaching might elicit fears of judgment and reprimand. Nothing could be further from the truth. No one is going to be critiquing your performance. There are no laps or pushups for failure to execute the coach's commands. No one is going to tell you what the next play is or even what your goal is. Making the coach or the team look good is not the goal, though it may be a side effect. [xxxvi]

With your coach, you'll analyze your own behavior. And you'll determine whether and when you succeed. As Dr. Collins continues, he lets us in on a few things Christian coaching is not: Christ-Centered coaching is not counseling, consulting, or mentoring. It is not therapy. In consulting and mentoring, the expertise lies in the consultant or the mentor and is transferred to the person. In coaching the expertise lies within you, the person being coached. The coach's role is to help you discover how to use more of your own potential and how to determine a strategy for which expertise is needed and doesn't already exist. The goal is to put your valuable skills, gifts, talents and personality to work-maximizing your strength to do what God wants you to do.[xxxvii]

"But those who wait upon the Lord shall renew their strength, they shall mount up with wings like eagles, they shall run and not be weary, they shall walk and not faint."[xxxviii] (Isaiah 40:31)

# THE ART OF ASKING QUESTIONS!

### The Top Ten Asking Mistakes:
In his book, Coaching Questions, pg. 12, Tony Stoltzfus gives us, what he says are the top ten asking mistakes made when talking with a client. He also provides a "Solution".

**Closed Questions:** Open questions have two benefits: they let the coach direct the conversation (because they can be answered in many ways) and they make the client think by eliciting longer answers. While most people will answer the occasional closed question as if it were open, too many closed questions in a row will shut people down.

**Solution:** The suggestion is to convert a closed question to an open question. We are advised that first you should become fully aware of what you are asking. If you catch yourself before you've finished asking, stop and restate the question. You'll know a closed question because it can be answered with a simple "yes" or "no," like these examples:

    a. "Is there a way to do that and still keep evenings for family?"
    b. "Can you realistically take that on too?"
    c. "Could there be any other way to approach that?"
    d. "Do you have any other options?"

When you catch yourself in the act of asking a closed question, here is a quick technique for adjusting: restate the question, but this time beginning with the word "what" or "how". Here are the closed questions listed above, but now made open using this technique.

    a. "What could you do to still keep evenings for family?"

b. "How would your life change if you take that on too?"

c. "How else could you approach that?"

d. "What other options do you have?"

**Solution-Oriented Questions (SOQ):** A special kind of closed solution question. SOQs are pieces of advice with a question mark pasted on. We want to tell the client the answer, but we remember we are supposed to be coaching, so we give our solution in the form of a question:

a. "Shouldn't you check in with your boss before you act on this?"

b. "Could you do your jogging with your spouse?"

c. "Do you think that affirming the person would give you a better result?"

d. "Can you give her the benefit of the doubt on this one?"

"Should you, could you, will you, can you, are you" - if the second word is in the question is "you," you're in trouble.

**Solution:** Follow Your Curiosity on a practical level. SOQs usually originate in an intuitive insight: something the person says makes us curious, so (all in our own heads) we proceed to identify what we think the underlying problem is, create a solution, and then offer it to the person. The trick is to go back to the thing that made you curious in the first place, and ask about that. Often this involves broadening our SOQ (which focused on one potential solution) into an open question with many possible solutions. For instance:

a. Our insight on the first question listed above was wondering what the channels of authority in this organization are. So we might ask, "In your company, what kind of channels do you need to go through before you act on this?" (Notice how this question allows for other answers than just talking to the boss.)

b. On the second question, our intuition noticed that the client is an extrovert, yet all the potential exercise options were done alone. You might say. "I noticed that all your exercise options were solitary activities. How could you involve other people in your exercise routine?"

**Seeking the "One True Question":** One of the biggest stumbling blocks for beginning coaches is the quest for the Holy Grail: The question that will unlock the secrets of the universe for the client. Before each question there is a long, awkward pause while we search our minds for just the right thing to say- and meanwhile the momentum of the conversation is lost.

**Solution:** It's not the perfect question that makes the difference; you just need to help the person you are coaching think a little farther down the road than they will on their own. Trust the process to help the person, not the greatness of your insight. One excellent technique when you are starting out as a coach is to lean on a very simple query, like; "Tell me more," or "What else?" The benefit of these short-and-sweet questions is that they don't interrupt the person's thought process at all. Another great tool is the Observation and Question technique. Pick out the most significant thing the person said, repeat their exact words, and ask them to expand on it, like this:

"You mentioned that _____. Tell me more about that."

By varying the question (instead of "tell me more…" try, "Say more," or "expand on that," or "What's going on there?") you can use this technique over and over without sounding stilted. It's a great way to keep the focus on the client and not on your greatness as a coach.

**Rambling Questions:**  A variant of the "One Question" problem is the rambling question.  Some coaches can't stop themselves from asking the same question in three different ways, while stringing together five different nuances or potential answers along the way.  By the time the coach has finally articulated the question.  The client is confused about what to answer and any conversational flow is lost.

**Solution:**  The propensity to ramble can usually be overcome in one of two ways.  First, some coaches do this because they are still figuring out what they want to ask while they are asking.  The solution is simple; allow it to be silent for a moment or two while you formulate the question.  Our discomfort with silence is leading us to jump in before we are ready to ask.  When you start doing this, you'll often find that a little silence will lead the client to continue to process without you asking any questions at all.

   The second common cause of rambling is that we are overly concerned that our question be fully grasped.  Our need to be understood comes from trying to lead the person down a particular path (in other words, we are in a telling mode).  Let go of your agenda, ask the question once, stop, and see where the person chooses to take it.  Often the most exciting coaching moments come when the client doesn't understand what you are asking for!

**Interpretive Questions:**  Sometimes just by asking a question we put a spin on what the client is saying.  For instance, a client says, "I'm finding it rough lately to want to get up on Monday mornings. I'm frustrated with my current project.  I'm not getting the support I need, and I keep finding myself looking at the clock and wishing the day was over."  A response like, "How long have you hated your job?" is likely to get a reaction from the client ("Wait minute – I never said I hated my job…!") The reason? Our coaching question reveals our interpretation of what the client said. We don't know yet whether this person hates his job, dislikes it, or even loves it. We only know what the client said. Interpretive questions erode trust (because they put something on the client) and block the conversational flow as the person responds to our analysis.

**Solution:** Interpretative questions are easy to correct. Simply make a habit of incorporating the client's own words in your question. For the example above, we might ask, "How long have you been frustrated with your current project?" or "What kind of support do you need that you are not getting?" or "What triggers you looking at the clock and wishing the day was over?" Asking in this way prevents the client from reacting to your spin and keeps the conversation moving in a productive direction.

**Rhetorical Questions:** Although posed in question form rhetorical questions are actually statements (often emotional or judgmental) of your own opinion of the situation:
  a. "What were you thinking?"
  b. "Are you really going to throw away your career like that?"
  c. "Isn't that just a cop-out?"
  d. "Wouldn't you rather get along with your spouse?"

Since we aren't really asking for the other person's opinion, these questions evoke either no response or just a defensive one. Rhetorical questions are generally a sign that you've made a judgment or developed an attitude about the person you are coaching.

**Solution:**   Eliminating rhetorical questions requires a change in attitude toward the client.  One way is to get in touch with what is going on inside you, and how this situation is pushing your emotional buttons.  A second approach is to renew your internal picture of the client's potential and ability.  Spend 15 to 20 minutes on these reflection questions to reorient yourself around believing in the client.

    a.    "Why am I forming judgments here?  How is focusing on the negative in this person meeting my own needs?  What can I do about that?

    b.    "Could I be wrong about the situation?  What am I missing?"  See if you can construct two possible scenarios where the client's point of view is more valid than your own.

    c.    "What potential ability and wisdom do I see in this person?  What can she/he become?

**Leading Questions:**   Leading questions are ones that subtly point the client to a certain answer:  the one the coach (knowingly or unknowingly) wants.  While rhetorical questions are blatantly biased, with leading questions you do not even realize you are propelling the conversation in a certain direction.  What response do you think the coach wants in the following examples?

    a.    "How would you describe that feeling, discouraged?"

    b.    "We've spent a fair amount of time processing this over the last several weeks:  are you ready to make a decision on that now?"

    c.    "Do you want to stay with this organization you've invested so much in?"

    d.    "It seems like this option would feel good today, but the other would provide lasting satisfaction.  Which one do you want to choose?"

**Solution:** Multiple Options, Or the Opposite: When you catch yourself in the act of asking a leading question, you can redeem it by creating multiple solutions. Take the leading question (like, "Name that emotion: are you disappointed?"), and then add several more options on the end: "...are you disappointed, excited, upset, or what?" With multiple options, the client has to choose how to respond, instead of taking the easy way out and just agreeing with you.

Another excellent technique is one I call "Or the opposite". If you realize you've just asked a leading question (i.e. "If you take this new position, will it take time and energy away from your family?"), paste on an "or," and then ask the opposite: "...Or will this open up doors to get you the kind of family time you truly want?"

Part of what makes these two techniques so useful is that you only have to change the very end of the question. You can realize you are asking a leading question midway through, and still change it on the fly without the client ever knowing what happened.

**Neglecting to Interrupt:** No, that's not a misprint. Being too timid to interrupt and refocus the conversation is more of a problem for beginning coaches than interrupting too much. While some clients speak concisely, others can go on for ten minutes every time you ask an open question. Too much irrelevant detail slows progress and blurs your focus.

**Solution:** Part of your job as a coach is managing the conversation, so when you see the client bunny-trailing, interrupt with a question that brings things back to focus. A pro-active step is to openly discuss the rambling issue and secure permission to interrupt when needed.

    a.   "It caught my attention when you mentioned that

_____, let's come back to that."

b.  "You are pretty good at expressing yourself. Would you mind if I interrupt occasionally to keep us on track so that we can make the most of our time?"

The other side of the Interruption coin is that for some of us (often the most verbal or relational personalities) interrupting is a habit we aren't very aware of.  Frequent interrupters tend to be perceived as dishonoring and frustrating to talk to – not the kind of image you want to cultivate as a coach!  Are you an interrupter?  If you want to find out, here's a revealing exercise.  First, record one of your coaching conversations.  Then fast-forward to the middle (by then you'll have forgotten you're recording yourself), listen to the tape, and make a note every time you hear each of the three following things:

a.  Interruption:  I interrupted or made a comment while the client was still talking.

b.  Talking Over:  I kept talking when the client tried to interrupt me; or when we both started simultaneously, I failed to defer to the client.

c.  Talking For:  I finished the client's sentences for him.

**The Solution:**  A simple discipline you can practice to break an interrupting habit is to make a commitment that when you are coaching you will count off two seconds ("one, one thousand; two, two thousand") after the client has stopped speaking before you reply or ask a question.  If the person begins speaking again before the two seconds is up, good!  Your goal as a coach is not to interject your ideas, but to help the client explore and implement their own.

Try to refrain from asking "Why" Questions.  "Why" questions tend to make people clam up because they challenge motives.

When you pose a question like, "Why did you do that?' you are asking the client to defend and justify his actions – so don't be surprised if they get defensive!

    a.   Why did you turn down that job"
         Better: "What factors led you to turn down the job?"

    b.   "Why do you think she'd respond like that?"
         Better: "What's causing you to anticipate that response?"

    c.   "Why can't you talk to him about that?"
         Better: "What do you need to talk to him about that?"

**Coaching Questions:** When used properly, coaching questions can be a great way to take everyday conversations from surface to significance. The way and manner of asking questions can be an important factor in initiating a conversation. As you begin your conversation, instead of asking, "How are you?" or "What's new with you these days?" and getting the standard replies, take a risk and ask about something you really care about. Give it a try.

# THE PROFESSIONAL LIFE COACH

In his book, The Dream Giver, Bruce Wilkinson relates a captivating tale of a person he refers to as a "nobody person" named Ordinary, who leaves the Land of Familiar to pursue a Big Dream that was given to him by the divine Dream Giver.  It was not easy at all for Ordinary to leave his Comfort Zone, and get past the Border Bullies, and all of the fierce Giants in the Land that were blocking the way.  As he traveled along through this vast wasteland, it became an effort just getting through the vast expanse of seemingly unimportant nothingness, before being able to reach the Land of Promise.  Wilkinson invites his readers to let him be their Dream Coach who, if they desire, may use the pages of his book to help themselves and other Dreamers move forward in their journey.  In this book, he sets the stage of the epic story of the Hebrews' journey out of slavery in Egypt, on into freedom in the Promise Land.  The pattern that is depicted for us reveals a pattern that is to be repeated time and time again throughout the Bible, whenever God's people reach for their Dream, an attempt at doing great things for Him.  In almost every instance, they:

   a.  Become aware of a personal Dream or calling and then decide to pursue it.
   b.  Face fear as they leave a place of comfort.
   c.  Encounter opposition from those around them.
   d.  Endure a season of difficulty that tests their faith.
   e.  Learn the importance of surrender and consecration to God.
   f.  Fight the Giants that stand between them and the fulfillment of their Dream.
   g.  Reach their full potential as they achieve their Dream and bring honor to God.

The good news for every Dreamer is that each stage or obstacle along the journey is intended not to block our dream but to help us break through to the fulfillment of God's promises. [xli]

As we consider Mr. Wilkinson's offer, it may be an excellent choice to suggest his book to anyone who may be considering getting involved with coaching. The story of Ordinary paints a vivid picture of what could be on the road waiting for anyone who would dare to believe that God has a plan for their lives, and that He guides their way, as they proceed on their journey. This guidance may come in many and various ways.

When we first learn about coaching, as we begin to understand how coaching is played out, we may get excited, and may want to get involved, even, in becoming a professional coach ourself. The thought of being someone who helps others in reaching their dreams, can be a very exciting prospect. Now, may be a time to discover ways and means of following your "Big Dream". Maybe the time is right to be asking yourself, "Is the Life Coaching profession right for me?

"Look into your past and look around your present and you will begin to see the coaches who help make you healthy and whole… They are just people at the right place at the right time with a passion to guide others through the ambiguities of living." [xlii] Thomas Bandy, author of Coaching Change.

## Life Coaching as a Profession:

As you consider Life Coaching as a profession, it would be well, at this time to take a look at the degree of passion that may be welling up, as your mind considers coaching. You see, passion is one of the strongest factors underlining our motivation and our energy as we consider proceeding into any of life's purposes. Passion is the energy of emotion that will define what we really care about, and what we will energetically pursue in our life. Check your passion factor before proceeding. This is the primary factor that urges us to do something. Without the dynamism of passion, we likely will never engage in our calling, with the drive and enthusiasm necessary to succeed at it.

A good starting place for working at, and, understanding passion, is the baseline of your assessment, as you begin your assignment with the client. Again, this is to be designed in a way that will help the client to understand and identify what they already know, and where more work in that area could be profitable. [xliii]

Professional leadership coaching takes time, commitment, energy and, once again, passion. Leaders who coach, must make the hard decisions, that enable them to carve out the time needed to invest in others. It is very difficult to develop this coaching mind-set and put it into practice if you are leading a large church or other organization, are busy managing a family, or are consumed with a hectic career. Indeed, there is evidence that successful, high-energy leaders rarely are able to adjust to making the changes necessary to become successful life coaches. So, from this, comes a whole new mushrooming profession arising to give coaching – usually for a fee – to those who seek guidance from someone with greater experience and objectivity. These professional coaches, who are cropping up, are mostly outsiders, with whom people inside the business world are frequently consulting. Business coaching such as this may not happen often in the church, but the broader issue of life coaching has tremendous potential. It can help transform Christian leadership, by moving it away from top-down managing, and into a coaching style of leadership, a leadership style that Jesus demonstrated, and, seems to be emerging today as the style many of today's generation appear to prefer.

# PASTOR/COACH/COUNSELOR/ CLIENT RELATIONSHIP

Ideas, thoughts and relationships are like paintings, they may be of the rare, fine art type, or they may be the everyday, familiar, garden variety. We all have thoughts. We all have relationships, as well as friends. So often, when leaders are first introduced to the idea of coaching, they look at the relational element and think, "Hey, I already know about that, we already do that – no big deal!!" Unfortunately, the statistics belie that view. There are a number of relational statistics regarding church pastors, indicating that as much as sixty percent of pastors in the United States don't feel they have anyone in their life they can honestly talk to about their job. And yet, another study found that even a higher percentage, seventy percent, do not have a close friend, a confidant or mentor. Three quarters of all pastor couples, will spend less than one evening a month engaging in purely social interaction with other couples. A full ninety percent said, the hardest thing about ministry, is dealing with uncooperative people. We're not as good at relationships as we think we are.

To say the least, coaching relationships are extraordinary, influential, life changing partnerships. As you consider your life, where you've come from, what you've come through, you might be thinking of an influential person in your life; someone who, at one time in your life, really believed in you, in an extraordinary way, a way that influenced you in a way that made a big difference in your development. Maybe it was a teacher who took that extra time to work with you to catch you up with other students, who sponsored you, or a church leader, a Sunday school teacher, who reached out and mentored you.

My mind goes back to my 4th grade teacher who took a special interest in me, and worked side by side with me. She assured me, I could do anything in life that I set my mind on doing. Also, there was a wonderful Pastor who took me by the hand, and led me through some tough spots in my life, and introduced me to Liberty University.

Increasingly, today, and into the future, coaching is rapidly expanding from a relationship between two people, to team, to small group, and peer approaches, between pastors, deacons, counselors, Sunday school teachers, board members, and others. One trend in coaching that is coming to the surface, is, working with a team of people simultaneously. This may include small groups, boards, and even whole congregations. Peer coaching also involves more than two people, but focuses on equipping team members, class participants, or church members to coach one another. This is like the lay counseling that has been effective for many years in the church. It works in a similar way, as leadership training programs teach managers, and others to use coaching in their day-to-day leadership as they work with others. [xliv]

The discipline of coaching is moving beyond professionalism, and into mainstream relationships. Much of the discussion that is now taking place within the coaching community is about professionalism of coaching by trained and certified coaches, for service, in return for payment.

## Coaching as a Ministry:

There may be another way you may consider looking at coaching, other than being a professional coach. What if, you were to see coaching as a ministry, as a way to serve others, to express your spiritual gifts, to contribute to your church and serve Christ? What if your goal is to use coaching methods in your work, and life, but without any intentions of calling yourself a coach? Is there a place for you in the coaching revolution?

According to Dr. Gary Collins (in his book, Christian Coaching), he says, that he believes there is a place for you, despite the challenge involved. He asked that we consider other fields that have come on the scene, such as; counseling, psychology, and other mental health professions. As each has emerged as a specialty with high standards for training, rigorous guidelines for credentialing, in the United States, as well as many other countries, legal restrictions on who is to be licensed to practice in exchange for a fee is being considered. He goes on to let us know that this does not limit anyone from informally counseling friends, nor does this restrict any from counseling parishioners, or, teachers from counseling students. The professional and legal restrictions do not apply as long as the people who counsel do not identify themselves as professionals, or, charge a fee. This is likely, also to be true of coaching should it become more professionalized and licensed.

# HELPING THE CLIENT REACH HIS/HER GOALS

It takes courage to dream, it takes courage to be vulnerable. Openness takes courage. As a coach we must interact with the client in a way that would affirm him or her to be vulnerable and to be open in their conversation about their dreams and aspirations. As the relationship starts to build between the client and coach, it will become necessary for the coach to gently probe further, in an attempt to get a clearer picture of the client's desires, as well as their passions.

As we consider this relationship, we must be careful not to fall into the trap, of, too quickly beginning to formulate ideas of, or, come to a conclusion as to what should be done and how to make it happen. We must guard against allowing that to take place; there is a possibility that it could take place, even while the client is in the process of sharing their dream. Resist the temptation of formulating, or, engineering strategies in your head, and getting this accomplished without enough input from the client. In ministry, this may become a temptation, as we may feel we have grown in maturity, and now, it is possible to have the idea that with all this experience, we now have the spiritual discernment that allows us to rapidly pinpoint another person's needs and abilities, and quickly prescribe an ideal solution. In this way of thinking, the more mature or "spiritual" we are [or think we are], the more may be our desire to intervene. "If people would only follow our godly counsel and focus on the important issues we've confronted them with, they'd be able to live victoriously".

As a coach, we must understand the client-centered approach. Coaching is based on internal motivation. The biggest obstacle to fulfillment of life desires, aspirations, wants and growth change may well be motivation. You, as a coach, can come up with great ideas for how to make a client's life better, but if that person isn't looking to change in that area, proposing it may likely be a complete waste of time. An excellent model of good coaching is to look to the client to set the agenda and solve the problems.

Tony Stoltzfus, gives us some very compelling reasons why a coach would want to allow a client to set the agenda. He gives us a list of 5 questions we can ask ourselves that will help us understand why the client should be the one to set the agenda.

a.  "Who will God speak to the 'firstest and the mostest' about a situation?"
    Coach or Client?

b.  "Who has the most information about the issues, decision or situation?"
    Coach or Client?

c.  "Who is most affected by the outcome of the situation?"
    Coach or Client?

d.  "Who has likely invested more time prayer and thinking over the situation?"
    Coach or Client?

e.  "Who has the most responsibility to take action in this situation?"
    Coach or Client?

Hopefully here, we can readily see that the person with the most information, with the most authority, the most responsibility and investment, is not the coach, but the client. Likely, this is also the one who God speaks to first. The client has more information about the situation at hand, and has likely invested more time and energy in his or her life than anyone else, and that includes the coach. Therefore, it is only natural to let the client set the agenda. Coaches do not direct the client; instead they help the client succeed at directing themselves.

# ALLOWING THE CLIENT TO
# SET THEIR OWN GOALS

As you begin meeting one-on-one with the client, your first
step will be to build a relationship.  Over time your conversation
will begin to include elements of skill development that you have
gleaned from your getting to know the wants, needs, aspirations, and
passion of the client.

Here are some very good guidelines to consider as you make
preparation for getting started using effective interacting techniques,
in the use of conversation.  Always remember that it is the client
that must initiate the actions to be taken, it is up to the coach to
encourage but not press.

The goal-setting process may differ from client to client but
usually goes through similar steps.

1.  Step one.  Clarify and agree on the end result (the desired
    outcome)
2.  Step two.  Put this on paper.  What you write can be revised
    later.
3.  Step three.  Start the desired outcomes and then, working
    backward, mutually brainstorm about some
    possible interim goals.
4.  Step four.  Agree about which of these alternative interim
    goals you will pursue.  Recast each of these as
    SMART goals:  specific, measurable, attainable,
    realistic, and with a time frame.
5.  Step five.  Arrange the agreed-upon goals in order of priority
    from the first and most realistic to the end result.

6. Step six. Write down indicators that will show clearly when each goal has been reached. Do this with at least the immediate goals. The others can come as you get closer to the end goal!

7. Step seven. Put this list on paper. Put it into a table. [xlvi]

We as Christians are never to forget, that God's plans very often evolve. We don't always see the whole picture at the beginning. We might not be able to fill out the entire seven-step program detailed in a chart, in detail from the start. When Moses stood in front of the burning bush, he got a partial picture of what was coming, but God did not reveal the entire strategy in detail. He said, "So now go, for I am sending you to Pharaoh. You must lead my people Israel out of Egypt" [xlvii] (Exodus 3:10). Moses was told to assemble the elders and he was given words to say. He was instructed to go to the king of Egypt, and to relay what God had commanded him. Moses was clear that the end result was to settle in the Promised Land, but initially he saw only the immediate goals. The overall plan unfolded in greater detail as he went.

The goal of stretching is to get people thinking in new ways, coming up with new options. Sometimes coaches can stimulate clients with questions like:

a. Imagine that you have achieved your goal. What does this look like?

b. Imagine yourself in the future and tell me how you got there.

c. If money or time were not limits, what would you do now to move forward?

d. Be creative, and tell me what measures you could draw on to help you move ahead.

e. What might change around you in the future that you need to prepare for now?

f.    What might you do that is outside your comfort zone but that might get you closer to your goal?

*"Anyone can dabble, but once you've made that commitment, your blood has that particular thing in it, and it is hard for people to stop you,"*
*~ Bill Cosby, entertainer*

Once our coaching clients have clear goals and a plan for action, there must be a commitment to make everything work. The coach commits to sticking with the client, giving encouragement, and guiding the person; the person being coached agrees to take action to move ahead. Commitment implies that there is no turning back, so the coach may need to get specific answers to questions, such as:

a.    "How willing are you to commit now to this plan?"
b.    "If you don't feel ready to commit, how does the plan need to change so you will make a commitment?"
c.    "What are you going to do first?"
d.    "When will you start?"
e.    "When will you have it done?"
f.    "Who will you tell?" (Commitment is stronger when somebody else knows.)
g.    "Who will give you support and keep you accountable?"
h.    "On a scale one to ten, what is the likelihood you will do what you have agreed to do?"

Once the process gets started, review the progress often. If something is working, congratulate the person and encourage him or her to keep going. If a goal is not reached, discuss possible reasons for this and find ways to revive the plan so success will come on the next try. Coaches do not blame, scold, or judge; instead, they help in ways that are mentioned in the Bible. They encourage, build up, confess, strengthen, show kindness, and care for one another. At times the coach will offer a gentle challenge, something like: "I notice that you did not follow through on what you promised, so I'm wondering what it would take for you to get there now?" Life coaching has no place for the tirades we sometime see in athletic coaches who stomp on the sidelines, scream, swear, intimidate, and shout names at their players on the assumption that this will motivate them to do better. At best the impact is temporary.

According to strategy experts, Larry Bossidy and Ram Charan, "No matter how well you exercise, the risk of failure increases markedly when the ideas you develop don't fit with your existing capabilities or force you to acquire those capabilities at too high a cost." [xlix]

"While stretch goals can be useful in forcing people to break old rules and do things better, they're worse than useless if they're totally unrealistic."

What is true of corporations can also apply to churches, community organizations, and individuals who come for coaching. Even as a coach encourages clients to stretch and have big dreams, sometimes his or her greatest contribution is to raise questions about whether the stated goals are beyond the client's capabilities. [1]

# COACHING FOR WIDOWED
# MEN AND WOMEN

As the population of America continues to age, as the "Baby Boomers" continue to reach that magical age of retirement, it would be well to consider the needs of this segment of our society. This segment of our population is far from unique, but they do bring with them into their retirement years some particular and at times, unusual needs.

**Size and economic impact of the "Baby Boomers":**

Seventy-six million American children were born between 1945 and 1964, representing a cohort that is significant on account of its size alone. In 2004, the United Kingdom baby boomers held 80% of the United Kingdom's wealth and bought 80% of all top of the range cars, 80% of cruises and 50% of skincare products. [li]

In addition to the size of the group, Steve Gillon has suggested that one thing that sets the baby boomers apart from other generational groups is the fact that "almost from the time they were conceived, Boomers were dissected, analyzed, and pitched to by modern marketers, who reinforced a sense of generational distinctiveness".[lii] This is supported by the articles of the late 1940s identifying the increasing number of babies as an economic boom, such as a 1948 Newsweek article whose title proclaimed "Babies Mean Business", or a 1948 Time magazine article.[liii]

The age wave theory suggests an economic slowdown when the boomers started retiring during 2007–2009. [lv] Projections for the aging U.S. workforce suggest that by 2020, 25% of employees will be at least 55 years old.[lvi]  Baby boomers control over 80% of personal financial assets and more than half of all consumer spending.  They buy 77% of all prescription drugs, 61% of over-the-counter drugs, and 80% of all leisure travel.

## Religion:

In 1993 Time magazine reported on the religious affiliations of baby boomers.  Citing Wade Clark Roof, a sociologist at the University of California at Santa Barbara, the articles stated that about 42% of baby boomers were dropouts from formal religion, 33% had never strayed from church, and 25% of boomers were returning to religious practice.  The boomers returning to religion were "usually less tied to tradition and less dependable as church members than the loyalists. [lvii]

## Aging and end-of-life issues:

As of 1998, it was reported that, as a generation, boomers had tended to avoid discussions and planning for their demise and avoided much long-term planning.[lviii]  However, beginning at least as early as that year, there has been a growing dialogue on how to manage aging and end-of-life issues as the generation ages.[lix]  A number of commentators have argued that Baby Boomers are in a state of denial regarding their own aging and death and are leaving an undue economic burden on their children for their retirement and care.

There are five basic phases to consider in any endeavor of life coaching, and this would certainly apply, and even more so to this over 60, age group;

   a. Discovering common threads of the talents and experiences developed in life through past experiences.

b. Examining and discovering one's spiritual gift as discerning the passions and desires planted in the human heart.

c. Finding courage enough to explore new experiences and opportunities with the recognition that the widowed person is one to be filled with "a new normal".

d. Prayerfully setting long term and short term goals toward those things where God may be leading.

e. Evaluating goals on a weekly basis to examine and overcome obstacles, doors clearly shut, or to move on to the next step with goals already met.

It is plain to see, that many of the "Baby Boomer" generation, consider life's challenges a bit different than did the generation before them. As they explore their new station in life, as they venture in and out of the many trials, crises and changes through this stage of life, as they are now left alone after 30-40 and at times 50 or more years of security in a life, together, with a loving husband or wife, now they find themselves feeling very much alone, and insecure.

Often, it is the destination that becomes the first decision on the priority list of things that need to be done. Destination is often based on a location, or a place that has always been on the want to experience, dream, or, "bucket" list. It may be focused on someone or something to visit or a project one always wanted to take on. It may even surround a business trip or the motivation may simply be to find a place to rest and relax.

It matters not what starts the impulse, it will always require the process of planning, exploration and elimination, time and effort. Be it the deserts of the Southwest, the deep South, city or country, or, even, someplace overseas, the possibilities can be far reaching, and, overwhelming at times, for someone who has neither "been there" nor, "done that".

A Christian Life Coach should encourage the client in the way that God leads. This way may lead the client through difficult times, using the unique gifts God has given to each of His Children, as "Born Again Believers". This may help us discern the threads of commonality on the road from our past, into our future.

Some in this age group may be drawn into the temptation to give way to fear, which may in turn, lead to isolation, hiding away from people, spending little time with relatives, and allowing their new situation to smother out their life. And, sad to say, this is far too common of an experience for many of the widowed. Isaiah 41:10, "So do not fear, for I am with you; do not be dismayed, for I am your God. I will strengthen you and help you; I will uphold you with my righteous right hand." [lvi] Even though there are many attempting to take advantage of the widowed, we can encourage with Scripture, not to fear. Once again from Isaiah, 35:4, "Be strong, do not fear; your God will come, He will come with vengeance; with divine retribution He will come to save you."[lxi]

As we are helping people discover the long term direction God has in store, many smaller tasks and goals are likely to have to be tackled first. There will likely be a need to de-clutter areas before the Lord can release the vision of a future plan. . Good management of time will be very beneficial through this journey. Remember; God is not surprised by all there is to take care of. He has a plan for the future and He even will reveal a good plan for tackling all the current tasks it is going to take to reach that future plan. Matthew 19:26, "With man this is impossible, but with God all things are possible". [lxiii]

A key to understanding the process of discerning God's will is to be active. In coaching we are taught that it is necessary to take an active role in discovering God's plan. Since God has a plan for our lives, but we don't quite know what it is, we begin praying. And that is exactly where we need to start. Step number two, is to exercise our faith, and listen for and to the ways God may be answering. It takes a measure of faith to exercise this step, faith to know without a doubt, that when we pray, God does indeed hear, and just as surely as He hears our prayers, He answers our prayers. Pray for eyes to see, ears to hear, wisdom to discern and to exercise patience when it's difficult to discern where and how God is answering prayer.

Always continue to ask deeper questions about any of the stumbling blocks that you run into along the way. Always pray, and continue to pray until you receive an answer.

Remember, life coaching, is, in a way, like coaching for a sport, in the sense that it is about developing ability, strength and perseverance. It's about learning how to play the game (to live life), developing the strategy to see, hear and work well while eliminating things that clutter and hinder along the journey. Continue to examine the road map, to determine when an adjustment should be made.

# UNDERSTANDING CHRISTIAN
# HEALTH AND WELLNESS

**Creation:** Starting in the first chapter of Genesis, in verses 27-31, after the creation of Adam and Eve, looking at their completeness, their emotions, their ability to think, reason, and their bodies, from their noses to their toes, and He said , "It is very good." The very first thing God teaches us is of primary importance, and that is, that He, that God, created all things. [lxiv] The second lesson is that God saw it as "Very Good." [lxv] (Genesis 1:31) As we look at this first book of the Bible, we see that it makes no distinction, in any way, that, some things of creation are very good, others are OK, and others are undesirable. God looked at all of His creation, the total completion of His creation, and as he surveyed it all, He declared that it was "Very Good." In the New Testament, Paul reiterates this point when he says, "For everything God created is good, and nothing is to be rejected". [lxvi] (1 Timothy 4:4) From the beginning to the end of the Bible a good creation, including good physical people, is a consistent theme.

But as we know, something dreadful happened, Sin came into the world. Man and woman disobeyed, and turned their back on God. This took place in the Garden of Eden, the very place that God had designed as a paradise, for both the man and his wife. Unfortunately, they ate the fruit God had declared off limits. So, consequently they broke their perfect relationship with God, with each other, and with all of creation. The painful reality of broken relationships soon became evident when Adam and Eve's son Cain killed his brother Abel (Genesis 4:8). [lxvii] The terrible implication of Adam's fall is not limited just to him. As the scripture points out;

"We all, like sheep, have gone astray" lxviii (Isaiah 53:6) and "All have sinned and fall short of the glory of God." lxix (Romans 3:23)

Rebellion against God causes people to be miserable, unhealthy, and unwell—but; There Is Hope. The Lord Jesus Christ says, "I have come that they may have life, and have it to the full." lxx Jesus died on the cross of Calvary, rose again to bring new life to all who would believe. God wants to change all things through Christ. lxxi Through Christ's redemptive work, as people place their faith and hope in Him, they are reconciled to God, and are challenged, as the children of God, to make all things as they were created, and, that is, to be – Very Good. Redemption means that all things are being made new in Christ. People still are inclined to reject God (to sin); even though sinning brings negative consequences. As we consider the "seven deadly sins" listed in the book of Proverbs, lxxii (Proverbs 6:16-19). Think about their everyday meaning in your life, how they affect our everyday activities, in us, as well as the lives of those around you.

## The Seven Deadly Sins:
   a. Pride
   b. Envy
   c. Anger
   d. Laziness and Apathy (Sloth)
   e. Greed and Materialism (Avarice)
   f. Overindulgence (Gluttony)
   g. Misguided or Sinful Desires (Lust)

The "seven deadly sins" cause much brokenness, heartache and grief, but the opposite of each sin, brings healing. Instead of the rot caused by envy, experience the peace that gives life to the body (Proverbs 14:30). lxxiii Instead of injury through furious irrational fits of anger, and loss of relationships, experience healing through gentle, irrational love and forgiveness, as God loves and forgives you (Matthew 6:12; Ephesians 4:32). [lxxiv] Instead of feeling unwanted, or, experiencing obesity caused by laziness, experience the promise of fullness in Proverbs 13:4, "The desires of the diligent are fully satisfied." [lxxv] Instead of being greedy for self-serving riches, live simply. Trust the scripture that says in Philippians 4:19, "God will meet all your needs according to His glorious riches in Christ Jesus," Romans 6:13, "Do not offer the parts of your body to sin, as instruments of wickedness, but rather offer yourselves to God." Your body is so important to God that he refers to it as a temple for His occupancy, in the Person of the Holy Spirit, who is in you, that as a born again believer, you have received. 1 Corinthians 6:19-20, "Do you not know that your body is a temple of the Holy Spirit, who is in you, whom you have received from God? You are not your own; you were bought at a price. Therefore honor God with your body." God's providence for your body is found in various places throughout scripture, (Matthew 6:31-38) (Psalm 104:14-15). [lxxvi] God's concern for our body is very evident, as He instructs us from even before birth, at the time of conception, and continues all the way through our life, until our last breath is expended from our mortal body, as our spirit is received, back by Him. After, which, He provides for us, a new body, designed for our use, and is designed to live on eternally, to be ours forever. (See Appendix #2)

I've always liked to use the story of Alice's Adventure in Wonderland as an example of a lack of focus. When most people are on a mission, they know exactly where they're going, and are most often, focused on the task of getting there. But with Alice's case, it's a bit different, she was not at all focused, as she asked; "Would you tell me, please, which way I ought to go from here? The Cat answered her with, "That depends a good deal on where you want to go," As Alice replied, "I don't much care where-"And the Cat responded back with, "Then it doesn't matter which way you go," Alice had not finished her statement, and she continued with, "- so long as I get somewhere," the Cat ended here with, "Oh, you're sure to do that, if you only walk long enough." [lxxvii] As I consider this story, it always reminds me of the importance of asking questions correctly, as well as asking correct questions, ones that will help discover the direction we should be heading, as we, move, in pursuit of our life's desires. At times we may get side-tracked, and become overly influenced by the idea, of, "bigger is better", and to what extent materialistic gain may seem important. David Myers, (2006) a well-known writer on psychology, argues that as affluence increased in society, we see depression skyrocket here in North America: Today, More than ever, we have big houses and broken homes, high incomes and low morale.

Robert Putnam, in his paper prepared for the American Sociological Review, asked a penetrating question; why do people watch the TV show "Friends" instead of having friends? And in his research, he made some important general observations. In his research, comparing survey responses found in 1985 to responses found in 2004, he states that researchers found, the number of people saying there is no one with whom they are able to discuss important matters nearly tripled in 20 years. [lxxviii] It was stated that on average, the number of people discussing important matters with others, decreased from approximately three to less than two people during those same two decades.

Scripture speaks openly to Christians, who, like Alice, lack focus. The Bible warns us against being tossed around, to and fro, moving from one fad to another, but firmly encourages each of us to, lovingly, stand squarely with God (Ephesians 4:14-15). [lxxix]

It is clear, if God has a mission, and He does, it would be helpful and really quite beneficial for us, as His people to have a mission as well. If we are to honor God, our mission must be consistent with God's mission, and, we must seek for, and be determined to have our mission in life, lined up, as best we can, with God's mission. A part of God's Mission is found in Isaiah 9:2-7 [lxxx] and can be seen in Appendix 3.

As we consider our mission, it is vital to understand that a mission needs to be something that resonates from deep within us, not something superficial, that we devise quickly. In the Scriptures, the Gospel writer, Luke, stated that the purpose he has for recording Jesus' words, is, "The Spirit of the Lord is on me, because He has anointed me to proclaim freedom for the prisoners and recovery of sight to the blind, to release the oppressed, to proclaim the year of the Lord's favor." [lxxxi] (Luke 4:18-19)

In his book, First things First, Steven Covey argues that "the power of transcendent vision is greater than the power of the scripting deep inside the human personality and subordinates it, submerges it, until the whole personality is reorganized in the accomplishment of that vision." [lxxxii] Once more, we look at Scripture, as it encourages people to "throw off everything that hinders and the sin that so easily entangles, and let us run with perseverance the race marked out for us" Hebrews 12:2. [lxxxiii]

As we continue looking into the Health and Wellness, we will, at this time look at;

### The Eating Habits in America:

**Dieting:** Women and men alike are experiencing more and more dissatisfaction with their bodies than ever before. American's spend

an estimated $50 billion a year on diets or diet-related products
(Berg, 1997[lxxxiv]; Fraser, 1997[lxxxv] ). Researchers have reported that
half of American women are on a diet (Cash & Henry 1995[lxxxvi]
; Smolak, 1996[lxxxvii]i). Twenty-five percent of men are on a diet.
According to the National Eating Disorder Information Center
(NEDIC), dieting is a futile, often harmful, process of restrictive
eating, usually caused by body dissatisfaction, preoccupation
with thinness, and the false belief that self-worth is dependent
on body size.[lxxxviii] Unlike healthy eating, which involves eating
well-balanced snacks and meals from a variety of foods that give
you energy to carry out your daily activities, dieting creates a
physiologically driven preoccupation with food and can have
devastating results, such as eating disorder, weight-loss surgery, and
even suicide. Most people who diet do not understand or believe
that healthy people come in all shapes and sizes.[lxxxix] The effects of
dieting include a preoccupation with food, irritability, depression
and social withdrawal, as well as lowered self-esteem when they
fail.[xc] In cultures where acceptance and self-esteem are often linked
to physical appearance, people seem increasingly to be judged
by the way they look. Information everywhere gives people the
impression they can shape their lives by shaping their appearance.
This reshaping of the body, usually, starts with dieting and maybe
experimenting with a new exercise program. This is strongly
attractive to people who feel unloved, ineffective, out of control, or
unlovable. They may try this in an attempt to take back control of
their life by controlling their physical appearance. [xci] Information
is available on the NEDIC website: www.nedic.ca/knowthefacts/
dietingfacts.shtmi.

**Causes of Body Image Concerns:** Many factors fall into play,
concerning body images, such as puberty, peer pressure, family
influences, the media, and gender differences. These factors

and more contribute to the development of the body image that concerns both men and women. There are several ways to overcome the negative thoughts and feelings a person may feel about their body. Martha Homme's, book "Seeing Yourself in God's Image", is an excellent resource with a step-by-step guide to help people overcome a negative body image and eating disorders. [xcii] The workbook outlines several conditions, as well as some useful steps that may be taken in order to minimize results. (See Appendix 4)

**Anorexia Nervosa:** This condition is characterized by a person's refusal to maintain a minimal body weight, an intense fear of gaining weight, significant disturbance in the perception of the shape of his or her body. In females, this may result in having no menstrual period. (American Psychological Association, 2004). [xciii]

**Bulimia Nervosa:** This condition is characterized by repeated episodes of binging (eating an abnormally large amount of food at one time) followed by behaviors designed to eliminate food from the body (e.g. self-induced vomiting, fasting, or excessive exercise.) The warning signs of bulimia include evidence of binge eating, like disappearance of large amounts of food in short periods of time, as well as purging behaviors. People with bulimia will frequently make trips to the bathroom after meals, use laxatives or diuretics, or follow excessively rigid exercise regimens.

**Binge Eating Disorder:** This is a recognized eating disorder that is characterized by frequent episodes of uncontrolled overeating (APA, 2004).[xcv] Researchers are just beginning to understand the causes and health consequences of binge eating disorder. Some of the warning signs of this disorder are; Eating frequently in large quantities; Feeling out of control and unable to stop eating; Feeling uncomfortably full after eating; Feeling guilty and ashamed of binge eating.

**Anorexia Athletica:** Compulsive exercising is not a recognized diagnosis in the same way that anorexia, bulimia, and binge eating disorder are. However, many people who are preoccupied with food and weight exercise compulsively to control weight in a misguided attempt to gain a sense of power, control, and self-respect. There are several warning signs of anorexia athletica, including exercising beyond the requirements for good health and having a fanatical obsession about weight and diet.

**Eating Disorders in the United States:** According to a number of surveys over the years, conservative estimates suggest that as many as 10 million females and 1 million males are struggling with eating disorders such as anorexia or bulimia, and as many as 25 million more people are struggling with binge eating disorder. (Hoek & vanHoeken, 2003; [xcvi] Shisslak, Crago & Easter, 1995; [xcvii] Furnham & Calnan, 1998; Neumark-Sztainer et al., 1999.[xcix] (See Appendix 5)

**God's Desire for His People:** Genesis 1:26 confirms that God created each person in His image, with an identity that is both physical and spiritual. Ephesians 1:5 says that Christians have the special privilege of being adopted into God's family. God wants people to know the Truth – Him. John 8:32 states, "Then you will know the Truth, and the Truth will set you free." God's truth is that He loves all people unconditionally. He wants people to know that. Even when they feel unlovable and worthless, they are worth so much in His eyes. This unconditional love, above everything, builds the foundation for the Christian's life. People who can't accept this love can't accept Christ, others, or themselves because God is love. (1 John 3:16) [c]

**Resist drastically reducing food intake:** Eating fewer than 1,000 calories a day could be setting yourself up for disaster, the change could likely be too drastic.  If you are interested in losing some weight, along with improving your lifestyle, the more desired process, would be to change in small incremental and sustainable changes.  In this way your change is more likely to become a permanent change as you continue to make your goals a reality in your quest for a life change.  The next step is to get a realistic assessment of your body composition.  If you have a healthy body composition and weight, proceed and enjoy what is happening, and maintain it.  The most important consideration is the improvement in the quality of your life by having a much healthier body composition and carrying around less excessive and unhealthy fat.

**Fight Heart Disease:**  It is remarkable, but the body needs very little "aerobic" exercise to substantially lower the risk profile for heart disease.  In one study of 2,678 men, those who walked only 30 minutes a day cut their risk for having a heart attack by almost 50 percent.[ci]

Several years ago some well-controlled scientific studies brought great attention to the benefit of eating oat bran to lower blood cholesterol.  The studies reported that by consistently consuming oat bran as part of the diet, the average person could expect a one percent drop in cholesterol. [cii]  We compare this to the average effect of cardiovascular exercise, which can lower total blood cholesterol by as much as 24 percent. [ciii]  Not only does consistent cardiovascular exercise tend to lower total blood cholesterol, it positively influences the ratio of "good" to "bad" blood cholesterol.

**Resting Heart Rate:**  In the process of continued cardiovascular exercise, the heart becomes stronger; it doesn't have to work as hard.  One reason for this is that as we exercise aerobically, the stroke volume increases.  Stroke volume is the amount of blood the heart pumps with each beat. The average adult pumps approximately 2.5 ounces of blood during each heartbeat. As stroke volume increases, the need for the heart to beat as frequently decreases. It's not uncommon for an untrained person to reduce the resting heart rate by 8 to 10 beats per minutes during the first 10 weeks of aerobic exercise, and may become as low as 35-45 beats per minute. [civ] This adaptation saves the heart about half a million beats each month.

**Frequency of exercising:** Exercise frequency may vary widely, but it has been shown that exercising three times a week for 30 minutes on alternating days is sufficient frequency to build aerobic fitness in most people. As your aerobic fitness improves, you may want to increase the number of sessions to between four and six per week. Increased frequency has some advantages. One study showed that six sessions per week were twice as effective as three at building cardiorespiratory fitness. [cv] Frequency, intensity, and time are interconnected. As your aerobic capacity increases, so will your ability to work longer, with more frequency, and with greater intensity.

**It Shapes-Your Body?** A common misconception among women is that if they lift weights they may end up with bulging muscles like a man's. Actually, women have nothing to fear. Women do have hypertrophic capacities. Hypertrophy means muscle enlargement and is the opposite of atrophy, or muscle shrinkage. However, women's capacity to enlarge their muscles is much more limited than men's. The main reason is hormonal; men have 20 to 30 times more testosterone than women do. High levels of testosterone help create a positive environment for building muscles. Anatomical differences also limit women's hypertrophic capacity.

**The Digestive System:**  The digestive system operates as an assembly line in reverse, taking whole foods and breaking them down into their chemical components.  Whenever we swallow, our digestive system starts to work, and goes on "auto pilot".  Because we are not in control of most of the digestive process, it is easy to overlook how much work the body does. Digestion begins in the mouth.  When we take a bite of food, your teeth and tongue begin to mechanically break it down into smaller units.  Saliva not only bathes your food with water, but it also allows you to taste because your taste buds work only when moisture is present. When the food has been reduced to a soft, moist mass, called a bolus, your tongue pushes it to the back of the mouth and into the pharynx, where it is swallowed.  For the fraction of a second it takes to swallow, your respiratory tract is closed, and you can neither breathe nor talk.  After you swallow, the rest of the digestive process is involuntary.  For the next two or three seconds, powered not by gravity but by muscular contractions called peristalsis, the bolus travels down the esophagus to the stomach to continue the digestive process.

**Antioxidants:**  Because of the vital benefits of antioxidants, I will very briefly explain them, as well as free radicals.  Free radicals are released during metabolism and stimulated by pollution, smoking, radiation, and stress.  Free radicals run throughout the body, attacking cells in the brain, heart, bloodstream, and immune system.  Antioxidants help minimize the damage caused by these free radicals.  Vitamins are among the most powerful antioxidants, along with carotenoids, flavonoids, and selenium (See Appendix # 7).

**Value of Human Relationships:** Relationships are without question, one of the most important things humans have. Nearly everyone, when it comes down to it, would rather give up careers, plans and ambitions, time and money, comfort and security, and even health than lose someone we love. It would be rare for a mother to run into a burning house to save her china instead of her children. A man in love wouldn't trade his fiancée for a new automobile. Relationships are true treasures, and they're delicate. Without skill, care, and nurturing they'll wither and die if they are neglected. But, with skill, love and continual nurturing, given the opportunity, they will grow and blossom.

**Relational Coaching:** Most students describe themselves as "good with people." (Walters and colleagues 2006).[cvi] More than 1,300 students who attended Christian colleges and universities were polled. Almost universally the students rated their ability to deal effectively with other people higher than every other measure of wellness surveyed (physical fitness, body image, weight management, stress, sleeping habits, and dietary behavior). (See Appendix 8.)

# THE FUTURE OF COACHING

As I consider the future of Christian Coaching, I would like to tap the resources of two well respected experts in the field of Life Coaching.

## First we have Dr. Tony Stoltzfus:

Dr. Stoltzfus lets us know that if we are serious about coaching in a professional sense, formal training is a must. Also, working with a coach trainer will help identify and rework your conversational habits and teach you to function out of a true coaching methodology. He continues, that many people (and ministries), who are "coaching" without formal training, are, in reality offering mentoring or disciplining and have not truly adopted a coaching paradigm. Then he lists for us a few Christian coaching training programs that he recommends as excellent.[cvii]

## Transformational Leadership Coaching:

Transformational Leadership Coaching (TLC) offers large U.S. based training ministries in multiple languages. The TLC professional program is a one year, 180-hour program with over 500 graduates in the U.S. and abroad, designed for those who want to coach for an income or as part of their job responsibilities. The curriculum, which can be taken at a distance, consists of three courses:

## Formation- Life Focus and Implementation.

In this program, each trainee meets one on one with a professional coach trainer every other week throughout the program. Trainees also meet regularly with a peer partner to practice relational and conversational skills. Each course also includes an interactive workshop focusing on practice and skill development. For more information you can check this out at www. TransformationalCoaching.com .

## The Institute for Life Coach Training:

ILCF offers a Christian Track Foundational Program, which is an ICF accredited program. It consists of 40 hours of classroom training via tele-classes and is designed for Christians who want to start a coaching business. A background in "people helping" is required for admission. The training is parallel to ILCT's secular program but is led from a distinctly Christian perspective. For more information visit www.LifeCoachTraining.com

Stoltzfus also lists: The Christian Coach Training Institute (CCTI) www.ChristianCoachTraining.com and Career Coach Academy; www.CareerCoachAcademy.com

## Next is Dr. Gary Collins:

Christian University Professor and Best Selling Author, Dr. Gary Collins, believes that in time, Christian coaching will become better known and more widely accepted. A few years ago, coaching was identified only with athletics. This is not true anymore. Almost everybody knows about voice coaches and fitness coaches at health clubs. The media, education, and the arts know about coaching and so do many people in business. Executive coaching has grown in influence although only a few years ago it was likened to "the Wild West of yesteryear (where) the frontier is chaotic, largely unexplored, and fraught with risk, yet immensely promising." In the past decade, life coaching has extended its influence even though the promise of lucrative private practices for life coaching has proven to be more fantasy than reality. Christian coaching is growing as well, but church leaders sometimes are reluctant to jump onto what may seem like another fad, this one imported from the corporate world without much apparent relevance to ministry. In all of these areas, coaching principles are likely to be accepted more broadly as their relevance becomes more apparent and coaching settles in as a proven way to help people who want guidance but see no need for counseling. [cviii]

# GET OUT THERE AND
# MAKE A DIFFRENCE!

Learning the art of life coaching is, among other things, about discovering how to make mundane conversations extraordinary. It's training yourself to show respect, honor and belief in people. It's building the kind of relationships we long for. It's helping others to grow, fulfill their destinies in ways that, in many cases, will exceed even their own expectations for themselves.

What would it be worth to you to be able to significantly improve your relationship with your spouse or your kids? What about the performance on your team at work? What if it improved by even 15%? What difference would it make if the people you minister to, each week had a coaching support structure to provide the follow-up they need to succeed? What if you invested significantly in just ten to twelve other people in your lifetime, so that they accomplished twice as much in the kingdom of God as they could on their own?

Those are some of the things you may be able to accomplish through involvement in coaching. The future of the Christian coaching movement is very bright, with new coaches entering the field on a daily basis. New leadership models are emerging, new methods, new training, and new utilization of up-to-date technology. I am very excited about the potential of Christian coaching that I have discovered as I've researched and investigated this new emerging ministry.

It will be a must, that over the ongoing years, our current methods of coaching will have to be adapted to make them relevant. They will have to be acculturated and redesigned for domestic as well as for international use. The coaching area still is being shaped by older people, often dedicated people with years of experience. I can see it emerging as a field that increasingly will captivate the young, who often, are able to mold and adapt it into a tool that can reach a postmodern generation and be used by God to have a great impact.

Today, the area of Life Coaching is open, and can make a difference in the world, and now you can know the fulfillment that comes from serving others. The time is right for Godly men and women to be involved, working toward improvement, in helping others. The Apostle John sums his own lifetime of ministry, in this, (III John 1:4) "I have no greater joy than to hear that my children walk in truth." [cix]

# APPENDIX 1
## Spiritual Gifts & Definitions

| Spiritual Gift | Scripture Reference | Definition |
|---|---|---|
| 1. Administration | 1 Cor. 12:28, Romans 12:8, Titus 14:5 | This is the spiritual gift where God the Holy Spirit enables certain Christians to organize, administrate, and promote the various affairs of the local church's ministry to direct them effectively. A local church cannot grow beyond a certain point without the ministry of these individuals. |
| 2. Apostleship | Eph. 4:11, 1 Corinthians 9:1, 1 Corinthians 12:28, Acts 1:22 | This is the spiritual gift that was given at the onset of the church by Christ Himself with special power to charter the newly formed church. |
| 3. Discernment | 1 Corinthians 12:10, Acts 5:3-4, 16:16-18, 1 John 4:1 | This is the spiritual gift where God the Holy Spirit enables certain Christians to know without a doubt whether a statement or behavior is of God, Satan, or man. ( This gift was very necessary in the days before the Bible was completed.) |
| 4. Evangelism | Ephesians 4:11, Acts 8:5-23, Acts 21:8, Acts 8:26-40, Matthew 28:18-20 | This is the spiritual gift where the Spirit enables particular Christians to share the Gospel to unbelievers and burdens Christians about soul-winning. All Christians are called to witness for Christ whether they have this gift or not. |
| 5. Exhortation | Romans 12:8, Acts 11:23-24, Acts 14:21-22, Acts 15:32 | This is the spiritual gift where the Spirit enables certain Christians to deliver challenging and encouraging words. |
| 6. Faith | 1 Corinthians 12:9, Romans 5:1, Romans 12:3, Hebrews 11 | This is the spiritual gift where the Spirit provides Christians with great confidence to believe and expect great things from God. |
| 7. Healing | 1 Corinthians 12:9, 28, 30, James 5:13-16 | This is the spiritual gift where the Spirit uses certain Christians to restore physical or mental health to the sick or demon possessed. |

| | | |
|---|---|---|
| 8. Helps/Serving/ Ministering | Romans 12:7, 1 Corinthians 12:28, Galatians 6:1-2 | This is the spiritual gift where the Spirit empowers certain Christians to render practical help in both physical and spiritual matters. Serving one another, like evangelism, is a calling of all Christians, but there are some who have a special desire to serve, and receive great blessing from it. |
| 9. Knowledge | 1 Corinthians 12:8 | This is the spiritual gift where the Spirit gives certain Christians the supernatural ability to understand God's Word and to effectively communicate it to others. |
| 10.Mercy | Romans 12:8, Luke 10:30-37 | This is the spiritual gift where the Spirit enables certain Christians to minister to and have compassion for those who are suffering or afflicted. |
| 11.Prophecy | Romans 12:6, 1 Corinthians 12:10, 1 Corinthians 14:1-5, Ephesians 5:11, 1 Corinthians 14:30-33, 1 Peter 1:20-21 | This is the spiritual gift where the Spirit empowers certain Christians to received revelation of events in the future. |
| 12.Pastor/Teacher | Ephesians 4:11, 1 Peter 5:1-11 | This is the spiritual gift where the Spirit enables certain Christians to preach and teach the Word of God and to take responsibility for the spiritual welfare of a body of believers. |
| 13.Teaching | Romans 12:7, Ephesians 4:11 | This is the spiritual gift where the Spirit enables particular Christians to communicate and clarify the details of truths of God's Word for others to learn. |
| 14.Wisdom | 1 Corinthians 12:8, James 3:13-17 | This is the spiritual gift where the Spirit empowers particular Christians with a supernatural understanding of God's Word and the will to apply it to life situations. |

*Adapted from Gail Ruth Peterson* [cx]

# APPENDIX 2

**Transition at death:** 1 Corinthians 15:51-58, the Apostle Paul, through the inspiration of the Holy Spirit, "Listen, I tell you a mystery: We will not all sleep, but we will all be changed – in a flash, in the twinkling of an eye, at the last trumpet. For the trumpet will sound, the dead will be raised imperishable, and we will all be changed. For the perishable must clothe itself with the imperishable, and the mortal with immortality, when the perishable has been clothed with the imperishable, and the mortal with immortality, then the saying that is written will come true: 'Where, O death, is your victory? Where, O death is your sting?" The sting of death is sin, and the power of sin is the law. But thanks be to God! He gives us the victory through our Lord Jesus Christ. Therefore, my dear brothers, stand firm. Let nothing move you, Always give yourselves fully to the work of the Lord, because you know that your labor in the Lord is not in vain."

# APPENDIX 3

**God's Mission, In Part:** "The people walking in darkness have seen a great light; on those living in the land of the shadow of death, a light has dawned. You have enlarged the nation and increased their joy; they rejoice before you as people rejoice at the harvest, as men rejoice when dividing the plunder. For as in the day of Midian's defeat, you have shattered the yoke that burdens them, the bar across their shoulders, the rod of their oppressor. Every warrior's boot used in battle and every garment rolled in blood will be destined for burning, will be fuel for the fire. For to us a child is born, to us a son is given, and the government will be on His shoulders. And He will be called Wonderful Counselor, Mighty God, Everlasting Father, Prince of Peace. Of the increase of His government and peace there will be no end. He will reign on David's throne and over his kingdom, establishing and upholding it with justice and righteousness from that time on and forever. The zeal of the Lord Almighty will accomplish this." (Isaiah 9:2-7)

# APPENDIX 4
## Specific Treatment Goals for
## Different Eating Disorders

| | |
|---|---|
| Anorexia nervosa | Focus on restoring nutritional status, normalizing eating and exercise habits, and altering attitudes toward food and body size.<br><br>Concentrate on feelings about body image, weight gain, self-esteem, and identify development. |
| Bulimia nervosa | Focus on interrupting the binge-purge cycle, normalizing eating patterns, and altering attitudes toward food and body size.<br><br>Understand emotional problems and conflicts that may have originally contributed to the bulimic behavior |
| Binge eating disorder | Focus on normalizing eating patterns and interrupting the binging cycle.<br><br>Change attitudes toward food and body size.<br><br>Understand emotional problems and conflicts that may have contributed to the binging behavior. |
| Female athlete triad syndrome | Normalize eating patterns and exercise habits.<br><br>Alter attitudes toward food and body size.<br><br>Concentrate on feelings about body image, weight gain, self-esteem, and identity development. |
| Muscle dysmorphia | Normalize eating patterns and exercise habits.<br><br>Become aware of cultural demands for unrealistic body ideals.<br><br>Engage in activities that have nothing to do with food, weight, or exercise. |

*Adapted from Christian Paths to Health and Wellness* [cxiii]

# APPENDIX 5
## Physical Complications of Eating Disorders

| | |
|---|---|
| Anorexia nervosa | - Abnormally slow heart rate and low blood pressure, which means that the heart muscle is changing. The risk for heart failure rises as the heart rate and blood pressure levels lower.<br>- Reduction of bone density (osteoporosis), which results in dry, brittle bones.<br>- Muscle loss and weakness<br>- Severe dehydration, which can result in kidney failure<br>- Fainting, fatigue, and overall weakness<br>- Dry hair and skin, hair loss is common.<br>- Growth of lanugo (downy hair) all over the body in an effort to keep the body warm. |
| Bulimia nervosa | - Electrolyte imbalances that can lead to irregular heart beat and possibly heart failure and death. Electrolyte imbalance is caused by dehydration and loss of potassium and sodium from the body and is a result of purging behaviors.<br>- Potential for gastric rupture during periods of binging<br>- Inflammation and possible rupture of the esophagus from frequent vomiting<br>- Tooth decay and staining from stomach acids released during vomiting<br>- Chronic, irregular bowel movements and constipation as a result of laxative abuse; peptic ulcers and pancreatitis. |
| Binge eating disorder | - High blood pressure<br>- High cholesterol levels<br>- Heart disease as a result of elevated triglyceride levels<br>- Secondary diabetes<br>- Gallbladder disease |
| Muscle dysmorphia | - Side effects and complications from steroid use<br>- Side effects from the overuse of protein supplements (e.g., kidney failure)<br>- High risk for injury from long, exhaustive workouts |
| Female athlete triad/ anorexia athletica | - Abnormally slow heart rate<br>- Bone fractures<br>- Ammenorrhea (absence of menses)<br>- Osteoporosis and decreased bone density (which cannot be regained)<br>- Fatigue that can inhibit athletic performance and increase risk of injury<br>- Electrolyte abnormalities<br>- Depression |

# APPENDIX 6
## Determining Who Is at Risk for Eating Disorders

| | |
|---|---|
| Anorexia nervosa | - Mean age of onset for anorexia is 17 years; peak years are between 13 and 18<br>- Perfectionist behavior<br>- Low self-esteem<br>- Preoccupation with becoming thin<br>- Dieting practices such as skipping meals<br>- Too much concern for body weight and appearance<br>- Participation in certain types of sports that emphasize maintaining a certain ideal body weight and shape, like figure skating, ballet, wrestling, rowing, running, or gymnastics |
| Bulimia nervosa | - Age of onset is usually adolescence to young adult<br>- Persons who have engaged in repeated dieting practices without success<br>- A strong need for social approval<br>- Conflict avoidance<br>- Inability to identify and assert personal needs<br>- Inadequate coping skills<br>- High distress levels<br>- Heavy emphasis on thinness in the family<br>- Lack of clear identities for two or more people in the family and difficulty distinguishing   between their needs, feelings, opinions, and priorities<br>- Overprotective parents<br>- Lack of conflict resolution in the family |
| Binge eating disorder | - Harmful dieting practices, such as avoiding eating during the day, restricting food intake to a low amount and avoiding certain types of foods<br>- Low self-esteem<br>- Problems with assertiveness<br>- Mood swings<br>- Perfectionism<br>- All-or-nothing thinking<br>- High anxiety levels |
| Female athlete triad | - Dieting at an early age<br>- Unsupervised dieting<br>- Restrictive diets and weight cycling in association with energy deprivation<br>- Reaching menarche before being emotionally prepared (weight associated with maturity decreases effective performance)<br>- Choosing a sport to participate in before the body matures or choosing a sport incompatible with body type |
| Muscle dysmorphia | - Being overweight as a child<br>- Early history of dieting practices<br>- Participation in a sport that demands thinness<br>- Having a job or profession that demands thinness (*e.g., models, actors*) |

# APPENDIX 7
## Fat-Soluble and Water-Soluble Vitamins

| Fat Soluble | Major Functions | Important Sources | Signs of Deficiency | Effects of Mega Doses |
|---|---|---|---|---|
| Vitamin A | Maintains eyes, vision, skin, linings of the nose, mouth, digestive and urinary tracts, immune function | Liver, milk, butter, cheese, carrots, spinach, cantaloupe, other orange or dark green vegetables or fruits | Night blindness, dry skin, increased susceptibility to infection, loss of appetite, anemia, kidney stones | Headache, vomiting and diarrhea, dryness of mucous membranes, vertigo, double vision, bone abnormalities, liver damage, increased risk of miscarriage and birth defects, convulsions, coma, respiratory failure |
| Vitamin D | Aids in calcium and phosphorus metabolism, promotion of calcium absorption; develops and maintains bones and teeth | Fortified milk and margarine, fish liver oils, butter, egg yolks, exposure to sunlight | Rickets (bone deformities) in children, bone softening, bone loss, and fractures in adults | Calcium deposits in kidneys and blood vessels, causing irreversible kidney and cardiovascular damage |
| Vitamin E | Protects and maintains cellular membranes | Vegetable oils, whole grains, nuts and seeds, green leafy vegetables, asparagus, peaches; smaller amounts widespread in other foods | Red blood cell breakage and anemia, weakness, neurological problems, muscle cramps | Relatively nontoxic, but may cause excess bleeding or formation of blood clots |
| Vitamin K | Blood clotting; maintains bone metabolism | Greens, cereals, fruits, meats, milk products | Hemorrhage | Jaundice, inability to clot |

| Water Soluble | Major Functions | Important Sources | Signs of Deficiency | Effects of Mega Doses |
|---|---|---|---|---|
| Vitamin B1 (thiamin) | Converts carbohydrates into usable forms of energy; maintains appetite and nervous system function | Yeast, whole-grain and enriched breads and cereals, organ meats, liver, pork, lean meats, poultry, eggs, fish, beans, nuts, legumes | Beriberi (symptoms include edema or muscle wasting, mental confusion, anorexia, enlarged heart, abnormal heart rhythm, muscle degeneration and weakness, nerve changes) | None reported |
| Vitamin B2 (riboflavin) | Energy metabolism; maintains skin, mucous membranes, and nervous system structures | Dairy products, whole-grain and enriched breads and cereals, lean meats, poultry, green vegetables, liver | Cracks at corners of mouth, sore throat, skin rash, hypersensitivity to light, purple tongue | None reported |
| Vitamin B3 (niacin) | Converts carbohydrate, fat, and protein into usable forms of energy; essential for growth, supports skin, nervous system, and digestive health | Eggs, chicken, turkey, fish, milk, whole grains, nuts, enriched breads and cereals, lean meats, legumes | Peliagra (symptoms include weakness, diarrhea, dermatitis, inflammation of mucous membranes, mental illness) | Flushing of the skin, nausea, vomiting, diarrhea, changes in metabolism of glycogen and fatty acids, low blood pressure |
| Biotin | Energy metabolism use, synthesizes fat, amino acid metabolism | Widespread in foods | Abnormal heart action, muscle pain, fatigue, weakness | None reported |
| Pantothenic acid | Used in energy metabolism | Widespread in foods | Vomiting, insomnia, fatigue | Water retention (uncommon) |

| Vitamin B6 (pyridoxine) | Enzyme reactions involving amino acids and the metabolism of carbohydrate, fat, and nucleic acids | Green leafy vegetables, eggs, poultry, whole grains, nuts, legumes, liver, kidney, pork | Anemia, convulsions, cracks at corners of mouth, dermatitis, nausea, confusion | Neurological abnormalities and damage, depression, loss of reflexes, weakness, restlessness |
|---|---|---|---|---|
| Folate | Amino acid metabolism synthesizes RNA and DNA; synthesizes new cells | Green leafy vegetables, yeast, oranges, whole grains, legumes, liver | Anemia, gastrointestinal disturbances, decreased resistance to infection, depression | Diarrhea, reduction of zinc absorption, possible kidney enlargement and damage |
| Vitamin B12 | Synthesizes red and white blood cells; other metabolic reactions | Eggs, milk, meat, liver | Anemia, fatigue, nervous system damage, sore tongue | None reported |
| Vitamin C | Maintains and repairs connective tissue, bones, teeth, and cartilage; promotes healing; aids in iron absorption | Peppers, broccoli, spinach, Brussel sprouts, citrus fruits, strawberries, tomatoes, potatoes, cabbage, other fruits and vegetables | Scurvy (weakening of collagenous structures resulting in widespread capillary hemorrhaging), anemia, reduced resistance to infection, bleeding gums, weakness, loosened teeth, rough skin, joint pain, poor wound healing, hair loss, poor iron absorption | Urinary stones in some people, acid stomach from ingesting supplements in pill form, nausea, diarrhea, headache, fatigue |

# APPENDIX 8
# The Peacemaker's Pledge

As people reconciled to God by the death and resurrection of
Jesus Christ we believe that we are called to respond to conflict in
a way that is remarkably different from the way the world deals
with conflict. We also believe that conflict provides opportunities
to glorify God, serve other people, and grow to be like Christ.
Therefore, in response to God's love and in reliance on His grace, we
commit ourselves to respond to conflict according to the following
principles:

### 1. Glorify God
Instead of focusing on our own desires or dwelling on what others
may do, we will seek to please and honor God—by depending
on His wisdom, power, and love, by faithfully obeying His
commands, and by seeking to maintain a loving, merciful, and
forgiving attitude.

### 2. Get the Log Out of Your Own Eye
Instead of attacking others or dwelling on their wrongs, we
will take responsibility for our own contribution to conflicts—
confessing our sins, asking God to help us change any attitudes
and habits that lead to conflict, and seeking to repair any harm
we have caused.

### 3. Go and Show Your Brother His Fault
Instead of pretending that conflict doesn't exist or talking about
others behind their backs, we will choose to overlook minor
offenses and will talk directly and graciously with those whose
offenses seem too serious to overlook. When a conflict with

another Christian cannot be resolved in private, we will ask
others in the body of Christ to help us settle the matter in a
biblical manner.

### 4. Go and Be Reconciled

Instead of accepting premature compromise or allowing
relationships to wither, we will actively pursue genuine peace and
reconciliation—forgiving others as God, for Christ's sake, has
forgiven us, and seeking just and mutually beneficial solutions to
our differences.

By God's grace, we will apply these principles as a matter of
stewardship, realizing that conflict is an assignment, not an accident.
We will remember that success, in God's eyes, is not a matter of
specific results but of faithful, dependent obedience. And we will
pray that our service as peacemakers brings praise to our Lord and
leads others to know His infinite love.

---

[1] Matt. 5:9; Luke 6:27-36; Gal. 5:19-26.
[2] Rom. 8:28-29; 1 Cor. 10:31-11:1; James 1:2-4.
[3] Ps. 37:1-6; Mark 11:25; John 14:15; Rom. 12:17-21; 1 Cor. 10:31; Phil. 4:2-9; Col. 3:1-4; James 3:17-18, 4:1-3; 1 Peter 2:12.
[4] Prov. 28:13; Matt. 7:3-5; Luke 19:8; Col. 3:5-14; 1 John 1:8-9.
[5] Prov. 19:11; Matt. 18:15-20; 1 Cor. 6:1-8; Gal. 6:1-2; Eph. 4:20; 2 Tim. 2:24-26; James 5:9.
[6] Matt. 5:23-24; 6:12; 7:12 Eph. 4:1-3, 32; Phil. 2:3-4.
[7] Matt. 25:14-21; John 13:34-35; Rom. 12:18; 1 Peter 2:19; 4:19.

# END NOTES

i  (Agassi)Andre Agassi, Sports Illustrated, Quoted in Christian Life Coaching by Tony Stoltzfus

ii  (Bible, The Holy Bible (NIV), NIV 1978) 2 Peter 2:9.

iii  The Holy Bible (NIV) Hebrews 9:27-28.

iv  The Holy Bible (NIV) 1 Corinthians 3:16-17.

v  The Holy Bible (NIV) Romans 12:1-2.

vi  The Holy Bible (NIV) Ephesians 4:16.

vii  The Holy Bible (NIV) 1 Cor. 9:16; 2 Cor. 3:4-6; 2 Cor. 4:7-12; 2 Cor. 12:7-10.

viii  (Gary R. Collins P. D., 2009) Gary R. Collins, Ph. D., Christian Coaching, (Colorado Springs, CO: NAV PRESS, 2009), 12.

ix  Tony Stoltzfus, Christian Life Coaching, (Virginia Beach, VA: Coach22, 2009).

x  (Creswell, 2006) Jane Creswell, Christ-Centered Coaching, (St. Louis, MO: Lake Hickory Resources, 2006).

xi  The Holy Bible (NIV) Job 11: 1-5.

xii  (Bible, NKJV 1994) The Holy Bible (NKJV) Psalm 139:14-16.

xiii  The Holy Bible (NKJV) Song of Solomon 2:14.

xiv  The Holy Bible (NKJV) Romans 12:1-2.

xv  Ibid.

xvi  The Holy Bible, Matthew 25:14-30.

xvii  The Holy Bible (NKJV) James 2:17.

xviii  Stoltzfus, Christian Life Coaching.

xix  The Holy Bible, Luke 10:27.

xx  Stoltzfus, Christian Life Coaching.

xxi  The Holy Bible (NKJV) Proverbs 3:5

xxii  Stoltzfus, Christian Life Coaching, 191.

xxiii  The Holy Bible (NKJV) Judges 6: 11, 15, 27, and 36-39.

xxiv  The Holy Bible (NKJV) Judges 7:15.

xxv  The Holy Bible (NKJV) Judges 8:7.

xxvi  The Holy Bible (NKJV) Judges 8:12.

xxvii  The Holy Bible (NIV) 1 John 5:4-5.

xxviii  The Holy Bible (NKJV) Judges 6:14.

xxix  The Holy Bible (NKJV) 1 John 4:4.

xxx  (Maxwell) John C. Maxwell, (www.academyofcaptains.com).

xxxi  The Holy Bible (NKJV) Colossians 3:23.

xxxii  (Welch) Jack Welch (http://www.webcoachingsolutions.com/quotes.htm).

xxxiii  Collins, 17.

xxxiv  Ibid.

xxxv  The Holy Bible (NKJV) Jeremiah 29:11-14a.

xxxvi  Collins.

xxxvii  Ibid.

xxxviii  The Holy Bible (NKJV) Isaiah 40:31.

xxxix  (Stoltzfus, Coaching Questions, 2008) 17.

xl  (Wilkinson, 2003) Bruce Wilkinson, The Dream Giver, (New York: Multnomah Books, 2003).

xli  Collins, 297.

xlii  (Bandy, 2000) Thomas Bandy, Coaching Change, (Nashville: Abingdon Press, 2000).

xliii  Stoltzfus, Christian Life Coaching, 113.

xliv  (Gary R. Collins P. , 1988) Gary R. Collins, Christian Counseling: A Comprehensive Guide, (Dallas: Word Press, 1988)

xlv  (Stoltzfus, Christian Life Coaching, 2009) Stoltzfus, Christian Life Coaching, 115.

xlvi  Collins, Christian Coaching, 207.

xlvii  The Holy Bible (NIV) Exodus 3:10.

xlviii  (Larry Bossidy, Ram Charan, and Charles Burck, 2002) Execution: The Discipline of Getting Things Done, (New York: Crown Business, 2002).

xlix  Ibid.

l  Collins, Christian Coaching, 212

li  (Walker, 2004) Duncan Walker, "Live Fast, Die Old", BBC News site, Sept 16, 2004.

lii  (Gillon, 2004) Steve Gillon, Boomer Nation: The Largest and Richest Generation Ever, and How It Changed America, Free Press, "Introduction", 2004.

liii  (Babies Mean Business, 1948) "Population: Babies Mean Business", Newsweek, August 9, 1948. Retrieved January 26, 2007.

liv  (Baby Boom, 1948) "Baby Boom", Time, February 9, 1948. Retrieved 2007-01-26.

lv  (Economy faces bigger bust without Boomers, 2008) Economy faces bigger bust without Boomers, Reuters, Jan 31, 2008

lvi  (Safer and Healthier at Any Age: Strategies for an Aging Workforce: Economy faces bigger bust without Boomers, July 19, 2012) L. Casey Chosewood, (National Institute for Occupational Safety and Health. July 19, 2012).

lvii  (Kim, 2012) Susanna Kim, Half of Baby Boomers to Leave Inheritance to Kids, (ABC News Consumer Report 2012).

lviii (Sullivan, 2007) Andrew Sullivan "Goodbye to all of that", Theatlantic.com, Archived from the original (November 6, 2007) on August 18, 2010.

lix (Broder, 2007) John M. Broder, "Shushing the Baby Boomers", The New York Times. (January 21, 2007).

lx The Holy Bible (NIV) Isaiah 41:10.

lxi The Holy Bible (NIV) Isaiah 35:4

lxii Gail Ruth Peterson, Christian Life Coaching for Widowed Men & Women, (Gail Ruth Peterson/Kindle 2012).

lxiii The Holy Bible (NIV) Matthew 19:26.

lxiv The Holy Bible Genesis 1:27-31

lxv Ibid.

lxvi The Holy Bible (NIV) 1 Timothy 4:4.

lxvii The Holy Bible, Genesis 4:8.

lxviii The Holy Bible, Isaiah 53:6.

lxix The Holy Bible, Romans 3:23.

lxx The Holy Bible, John 10:10.

lxxi The Holy Bible, Colossians 1:19-20.

lxxii The Holy Bible, Proverbs 6:16-19.

lxiii The Holy Bible, Proverbs 14:30.

lxxiv The Holy Bible, Matthew 6:12; Ephesians 4:32.

lxxv The Holy Bible, Proverbs 13:4.

lxxvi The Holy Bible, Matthew 6:31-38 and Psalm 104:14-15.

lxxvii (Carroll, 1865)

lxxviii (Putnam, 2006)

lxxix The Holy Bible, Ephesians 4:14-15.

lxxx The Holy Bible, Isaiah 9:2-7.

lxxxi The Holy Bible, Luke 4:18-19.

lxxii (Steven Covey, A. Roger Merrill, Rebecca R. Merrill, 1994)

lxxiii The Holy Bible (NIV), Hebrews 12:2

lxxxiv (Berg, 1997)

lxxxv (Fraser, 1997)

lxxxvi (T. E. Cash, P. E. Henry, 1995)

lxxxvii (Smolak, 1996)

lxxxviii (Bear)

lxxxix Ibid.

lc Ibid.

lci Ibid.

lcii (Homme, 1999)

lxiii (Eating disorders: Psychotherapy's role in effective treatment., 2004) lciv  Ibid.

xcv  Ibid.

xcvi  (Hoek, H. W. & van Hoeken, D, 2003)

xcvii  (Shisslak, C.M., Crago, M., & Estes, L.S., 1995)

xcviii  (Furnham, A, & Calnan, A., 1998)

xcix  (Neumark-Sztainer, D., Story, M., Falkner, N.H., Beuhring, T., & Resnick, M., 1999)

c  (Bible, The Holy Bible (NIV), NIV 1978)

ci  (McKinnon, 1999)

cii  (Kerckhoffs, D.A., Hornstra, G., & Mensink, R.P., 2003)

ciii  (Hales, 2001)

civ  (Nieman, 2003)

cv  Ibid.

cvi  (Walters, P., Gustafson, J., Williams, B., & Carlson, K., 2006)

cvii  (Stoltzfus, Leadership Coaching, 2005) 297.

cviii  (Gary R. Collins P. D., 2009) 341.

cix  The Holy Bible (NKJV) III John 1:4.

cx  (Peterson, 2012) 16-17.

cxi  The Holy Bible (NIV) 1 Corinthians 15:51-58.

cxii  The Holy Bible (NIV) Isaiah 9:2-7.

cxiii  (Peter Walters, Ph. D. and John Byl, Ph. D., 2008) 50.

cxiv  (Peter Walters, Ph. D. and John Byl, Ph. D., 2008) 47.

cxv  (Peter Walters, Ph. D. and John Byl, Ph. D., 2008) 40.

cxvi  (Peter Walters, Ph. D. and John Byl, Ph. D., 2008) 171-172.

cxvii  (Peter Walters, Ph. D. and John Byl, Ph. D., 2008) 272.

# BIBLIOGRAPHY

Agassi, A. (n.d.). Sports Illustrated.

*Babies Mean Business*. (1948, August 9). Retrieved January 26, 2007, from Newsweek.

*Baby Boom*. (1948, February 9). Retrieved January 26, 2007, from Time.

Bandy, T. G. (2000). *Coaching Change*. Nashville: Abingdon Press.

Bear, M. (n.d.). *Dieting and Weight Loss Facts and Fiction*. Retrieved June 27, 2007, from National Eating Disorder Information Pamphlet, Toronto: www.nedic.ca/knowthefacts/dietingfacts.shtml

Berg, F. M. (1997). Afraid to eat: Children and teens in weight crises. *Healthy Weight Publishing Network*.

Bible. (NIV 1978). *The Holy Bible* (NIV). Grand Rapids: Zondervan.

Bible. (NKJV 1994). *The Holy Bible* (NKJV). Nashville: Thomas Nelson.

Broder, J. M. (2007, January 21). *Shushing the Baby Boomers*. New York Times.

Carroll, L. (1865). *Alice in Wonderland*. London: Macmillan.

Creswell, J. (2006). *Christ-Centered Coaching*. St. Louis, MO: Lake Hickory Resources.

*Eating disorders: Psychotherapy's role in effective treatment*. (2004). Retrieved June 28, 2007, from American Psychological Association: www.apahelpcenter.org/articles/article.php?id=50

*Economy faces bigger bust without Boomers*. (2008, January 31). Reuters.

Fraser, L. (1997). *Losing It: America's Obsession with \Weight and the i\ Industry the Feeds on It*. New York: Penguin BOoks.

Furnham, A, & Calnan, A. (1998). Eating Disturbances, Self-esteem, Reasons for Exercising and Body Weight Dissatisfactions in Adolescent Males. *European Eating Disorders Review*, 58-72.

Gary R. Collins, P. (1988). *Christian Counseling: A Comprehensive Guide*. Dallas: Word Publishing.

Gary R. Collins, P. D. (2009). *Christian Coaching*. Colorado Springs: Nav Press.

Gillon, S. (2004). Boomer Nation: The Largest and Richest Generation Ever, and How It Changed America. Free Press "Introduction".

Hales, D. (2001). *An Invitation to Fitness & Wellness*. Belmont, CA: Wadsworth.

Hoek, H. W. & van Hoeken, D. (2003). The Female Athlete Triad. *American Family Physician*, 3357-3370.

Homme, M. (1999). *Turning Point Workbook, Seeing Yourself in God's Image*. Chattanooga: Turning Point.

Kerckhoffs, D.A., Hornstra, G., & Mensink, R.P. (2003). Cholesterol-lowering Effect of Beta-glucan from Oat Bran in Mildly Hypercholesterolemic Subjects May Decrease When Beta-glucan is Incorporated into Bread and Cookies. *American Journal of Clinical Nutrition*, 221-227.

Kim, S. (2012). *Half of Baby Boomers to Leave Inheritance to Kids*. ABC News Consumer Report.

Larry Bossidy, Ram Charan, and Charles Burck. (2002). *Execution: The Discipline of Getting Things Done*. New York: Crown Business.

Maxwell, J. (n.d.). Retrieved from www.academyofcaptains.com

McKinnon, M. (1999). Walk Your Way to Total Health. *American Health*, 74.

Neumark-Sztainer, D., Story, M., Falkner, N.H., Beuhring, T., & Resnick, M. (1999). Disordered Eating Among Adolescents with Chronic Illness: Exploring the Role of Family and Other social Factors. *Archives of Pediatrics and Adolescent Medicine*, 871-878.

Nieman, D. (2003). *Exercise testing and prescription: A Health-related Approach*. Boston: McGraw-Hill.

Peter Walters, Ph. D. and John Byl, Ph. D. (2008). *Christian Paths to Health and Wellness*. Champaign, Illinois: Human Kinetics.

Peterson, G. R. (2012). *Christain Life Coaching for Widowed Men & Women*. Gail Ruth Peterson: Kindle.

Putnam, R. (2006). *Bowling Alone*. McPherson, Smith-Lovin, & Bradshears.

(July 19, 2012). *Safer and Healthier at Any Age: Strategies for an Aging Workforce: Economy faces bigger bust without Boomers*. National Institute for Occupational Safety and Health.

Shisslak, C.M., Crago, M., & Estes, L.S. (1995). The Spectrum of Eating Disturbances. *International Journal of Eating Disorders*, 209-219.

Smolak, L. (1996). Next door neighbors: Eathing disorders awareness and prevention puppet guide book. Seattle: *National Eating Disorders Association*.

Steven Covey, A. Roger Merrill, Rebecca R. Merrill. (1994). *First Things First*. New York: Simon and Schuster.

Stoltzfus, T. (2005). *Leadership Coaching*.

Stoltzfus, T. (2008). *Coaching Questions*. Virginia Beach, VA: Coach22.

Stoltzfus, T. (2009). *Christian Life Coaching*. Virginia Beach, VA: Coach22.

Sullivan, A. (2007, November 6). *Goodbye to all of that*. Retrieved August 18, 2010, from Theatlantic.com.

T. E. Cash, P. E. Henry. (1995). Women's Body Images. *Sex Roles* (33), 19-28.

Walker, D. (2004, September 16). "Live Fast, Die Old". BBC News.

Walters, P., Gustafson, J., Williams, B., & Carlson, K. (2006). What your students are really thinking. *Christian Society of Kinesiology Sport, and Leisure*. Boston.

Welch, J. (n.d.). Retrieved from http://www.webcoachingsolutions.com/quotes.htm

Wilkinson, B. (2003). *The Dream Giver*. New York: Multnomah Books.

www.ingramcontent.com/pod-product-compliance
Lightning Source LLC
LaVergne TN
LVHW021520080426
835509LV00018B/2584